Death & Dying
Opposing
Viewpoints

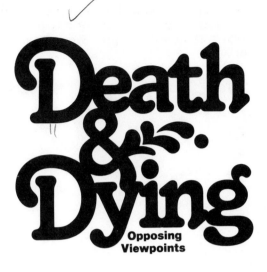

Death & Dying

**Opposing
Viewpoints**

David L. Bender
Richard Hagen

OPPOSING VIEWPOINTS SERIES

Greenhaven Press
577 Shoreview Park Road
St. Paul, Minnesota 55126

Library of Congress Cataloging in Publication Data
Main entry under title:

Death & dying.

(Opposing viewpoints series)
Bibliography: p.
Summary: Presents opposing viewpoints on the meaning of death, when it occurs, how to greet death, reacting to death, and life after death, through essays by a variety of authors. Includes discussion activities.
1. Death—Religious aspects—Comparative studies.
2. Future life—Religious aspects—Comparative studies.
3. Bereavement. [1. Death—Addresses, essays, lectures]
I. Bender, David L., 1936-   . II. Hagen, Richard. III. Title: Death and dying. IV. Series.
HQ1073.D39 1985   306'.9   85-8066
ISBN 0-89908-331-5 (lib. bdg.)
ISBN 0-89908-306-4 (pbk.)

CONGRESS SHALL MAKE NO LAW... ABRIDGING THE FREEDOM OF SPEECH, OR OF THE PRESS

first amendment to the U.S. Constitution

The basic foundation of our democracy is the first amendment guarantee of freedom of expression. The OPPOSING VIEW-POINTS SERIES is dedicated to the concept of this basic freedom and the idea that it is more important to practice it than to enshrine it.

TABLE OF CONTENTS

Page

the Opposing viewpoints series

THE IMPORTANCE OF EXAMINING
OPPOSING VIEWPOINTS

The purpose of this book, and the Opposing Viewpoints Series as a whole, is to confront you with alternative points of view on complex and sensitive issues.

Perhaps the best way to inform yourself is to analyze the positions of those who are regarded as experts and well studied on the issues. It is important to consider every variety of opinion in an attempt to determine the truth. Opinions from the mainstream of society should be examined. Also important are opinions that are considered radical, reactionary, minority or stigmatized by some other uncomplimentary label. An important lesson of history is the fact that many unpopular and even despised opinions eventually gained widespread acceptance. The opinions of Socrates, Jesus and Galileo are good examples of this.

You will approach this book with opinions of your own on the issues debated within it. To have a good grasp of your own viewpoint you must understand the arguments of those with whom you disagree. It is said that those who do not completely understand their adversary's point of view do not fully understand their own.

Perhaps the most persuasive case for considering opposing viewpoints has been presented by John Stuart Mill in his work *On Liberty*. Consider the following statements of his when studying controversial issues.

THE OPINIONS OF OTHERS

If all mankind minus one were of one opinion, and only one person were of the contrary opinion, mankind would be no more justified in silencing that one person than he, if he had the power, would be justified in silencing mankind....

We can never be sure that the opinion we are endeavoring to stifle is a false opinion...

All silencing of discussion is an assumption of infallibility....

Ages are no more infallible than individuals; every age having held many opinions which subsequent ages have deemed not only false but absurd; and it is as certain that many opinions now general will be rejected by future ages....

The only way in which a human being can make some approach to knowing the whole of a subject, is by hearing what can be said about it by persons of every variety of opinion, and studying all modes in which it can be looked at by every character of mind. No wise man ever acquired his wisdom in any mode but this....

The beliefs which we have most warrant for have no safeguard to rest on but a standing invitation to the whole world to prove them unfounded....

To call any proposition certain, while there is any one who would deny its certainty if permitted, but who is not permitted, is to assume that we ourselves and those who agree with us are the judges of certainty, and judges without hearing the other side....

Men are not more zealous for truth than they are for error, and a sufficient application of legal or even social penalties will generally succeed in stopping the propagation of either....

However unwilling a person who has a strong opinion may admit the possibility that his opinion may be false, he ought to be moved by the consideration that, however true it may be, if it is not fully, frequently, and fearlessly discussed, it will be a dead dogma, not a living truth.

I would like to point out to younger readers that John Stuart Mill lived in an era that was not sensitive to terms many people today consider sexist. The words *man* and *mankind* were often used in his work as synonyms for *people* and *humankind*.

A pitfall to avoid in considering alternative points of view is that of regarding your own point of view as being merely common sense and the most rational stance, and the point of view of others as being only opinion and naturally wrong. It may be that the opinion of others is correct and that yours is in error.

Another pitfall to avoid is that of closing your mind to the opinions of those whose views differ from yours. The best way to approach a dialogue is to make your primary purpose that of understanding the mind and arguments of the other person and not that of enlightening him or her with your solutions. One learns more by listening than by speaking.

It is my hope that after reading this book you will have a deeper understanding of the issues debated and will appreciate the complexity of even seemingly simple issues when good and honest people disagree. This awareness is particularly important in a democratic society such as ours, where people enter into public debate to determine the common good. People with whom you disagree should not be regarded as enemies, but rather as friends who suggest a different path to a common goal.

ANALYZING SOURCES OF INFORMATION

The Opposing Viewpoints Series uses diverse sources; magazines, journals, books, newspapers, statements and position papers from a wide range of individuals and organizations. These sources help in the development of a mindset that is open to the consideration of a variety of opinions.

The format of the Opposing Viewpoints Series should help you answer the following questions.

1. *Are you aware that three of the most popular weekly news magazines, Time, Newsweek,* and *U.S. News and World Report are not totally objective accounts of the news?*
2. **Do you know there is no such thing as a completely objective author, book, newspaper or magazine?**
3. **Do you think that because a magazine or newspaper article is unsigned it is always a statement of facts rather than opinions?**
4. **How can you determine the point of view of newspapers and magazines?**
5. **When you read do you question an author's frame of reference (political persuasion, training, and life experience)?**

Many people finish their formal education unable to cope with these basic questions. They have little chance to understand the social forces and issues surrounding them. Some fall easy victims to demagogues preaching solutions to problems by scapegoating minorities with conspiratorial and paranoid explanations of complex social issues.

I do not want to imply that anything is wrong with authors and publications that have a political slant or bias. All authors have a frame of reference. Readers should understand this. You should also understand that almost all writers have a point of view. An important skill in reading is to be able to locate and identify a point of view. This series gives you practice in both.

DEVELOPING BASIC THINKING SKILLS

A number of basic skills for critical thinking are practiced in the discussion activities that appear throughout the books in the series. Some of the skills are:

Locating a Point of View The ability to determine which side of an issue an author supports.

Evaluating Sources of Information The ability to choose from among alternative sources the most reliable and accurate source in relation to a given subject.

Distinguishing Between Primary and Secondary Sources The ability to understand the important distinction between sources which are primary (original or eyewitness accounts) and those which are secondary (historically removed from, and based on, primary sources).

Separating Fact from Opinion The ability to make the basic distinction between factual statements (those which can be demonstrated or verified empirically) and statements of opinion (those which are beliefs or attitudes that cannot be proved).

Distinguishing Between Prejudice and Reason The ability to differentiate between statements of prejudice (unfavorable, preconceived judgments based on feelings instead of reason) and statements of reason (conclusions that can be clearly and logically explained or justified).

Identifying Stereotypes The ability to identify oversimplified, exaggerated descriptions (favorable or unfavorable) about people and insulting statements about racial, religious or national groups, based upon misinformation or lack of information.

Recognizing Ethnocentrism The ability to recognize attitudes or opinions that express the view that one's own race, culture, or group is inherently superior, or those attitudes that judge another race, culture, or group in terms of one's own.

It is important to consider opposing viewpoints. It is equally important to be able to critically analyze those viewpoints. The discussion activities in this book will give you practice in mastering these thinking skills.

Using this book, and others in the series, will help you develop critical thinking skills. These skills should improve your ability to better understand what you read. You should be better able to separate fact from opinion, reason from rhetoric. You should become a better consumer of information in our media-centered culture.

A VALUES ORIENTATION

Throughout the Opposing Viewpoints Series you are presented conflicting values. A good example is *American Foreign Policy*. The first chapter debates whether foreign policy should be based on the same kind of moral principles that individuals use in guiding their personal actions, or instead be based primarily on doing what best advances national interests, regardless of moral implications.

The series does not advocate a particular set of values. Quite the contrary! The very nature of the series leaves it to you, the reader, to formulate the values orientation that you find most suitable. My purpose, as editor of the series, is to see that this is made possible by offering a wide range of viewpoints which are fairly presented.

David L. Bender
Opposing Viewpoints Series Editor

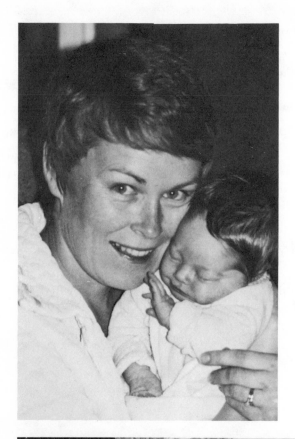

"a time to
be born,

a time to die."

DEATH: THE FINAL MYSTERY

As Henry Ward Beecher lay on his deathbed, he turned to his family and said: "Now comes the final mystery." Beecher was expressing a sentiment which has gnawed at humanity ever since the first cave dweller cried out fitfully at the prospect of his mortality. As Beecher so aptly expressed it, death is indeed the final mystery. Despite the claims of theologists of an after-life and the protests by atheists of nothingness, no one has ever been able to offer tangible and visible evidence of what follows this state of being which we call life.

Because death is an unknown quality, many people react to its inevitable coming with fear. In fact, much of Western society has, in a sense, institutionalized this fear by enveloping it in a shroud of silence. Robert Fulton, professor of sociology at the University of Minnesota and director of its Center for Death Education, described the thought and reality of death as being a "taboo" topic in contemporary society. He wrote: "No social institution or group has been free from the attempt to deny our mortality. In the home, at school, from the church pulpit to the 'slumber' room of the mortuary, we have attempted to shield ourselves from the prospect of our own death as well as from the death of others."

Today, however, attempts are being made to hold death to the light of day. Although we may speak of these attempts as representing little more than a grey, misty dawn, they none-theless appear to represent a process which may one day shatter the ageless "taboo". Theologians, teachers, newspaper columnists, physicians, and a host of other service oriented professionals, are exposing what appears to be an ever growing audience to the subject of death.

The purpose of this book is to present its readers a broad spectrum of issues relating to death and dying. Each issue is defined, explained and/or identified by a variety of viewpoints. Oriental and Western statements on the meaning of death and life after death are offered along with readings by Elisabeth Kubler-Ross, whose pioneering works on the subject have fired an international controversy. Death is personalized in chapters three and four, "How Should You Greet Death?" and "How Should You React to Another's Death?" Finally, the pressing issue of "Death Defined" is presented in four opposing viewpoints. The medical-legal problems raised by the question, "When is a person dead?", is especially relevant in a world where life-sustaining devices can keep the "all but dead" visibly alive. It is the hope of the editors that these readings will contribute not only to a better understanding of death, but also will play a small part in diminishing its accompanying "taboo".

Chapter

1

Death & Dying

What is the Meaning of Death?

" 'Lord Jesus receive my spirit.' For the Christian, death is precisely that, handing his spirit, his soul, his inner being over to Jesus."

A Christian View of Death

James Scully

The following viewpoint was taken from a pamphlet titled *Death and the Christian*, written by James Scully. Mr. Scully, a former Benedictine Priest, is the editor of Dove Publications at Peco Benedictine Monastery in Pecos, New Mexico.

Consider the following questions while reading:

1. The author claims that when the Christian thinks of death "he thinks first of all not of his own but of Jesus' death." What does he mean?
2. Why does the author say we have nothing to fear from death? Do you agree?

James Scully, "Death and the Christian". Published by the monks of St. Benedict's Abbey, Benet Lake, Wisconsin.

MEETING JESUS

"Lord Jesus receive my spirit."

These simple but exquisitely beautiful words of Stephen, uttered as his enemies were murdering him (Acts 7:59), sum up the whole theology of death.

For the Christian, death is precisely that — handing his spirit, his soul, his inner being over to Jesus.

For one who has been meeting the Savior by loving others and being loved by them, in the sacraments, in the New Testament, in prayer, death can no longer be a thing to dread. It is but the ultimate encounter with the person who loves him most deeply, the union that will never know even a moment of separation.

DEATH IS THE BEGINNING

When a Christian thinks of death, he thinks first of all not of his own, but of Jesus' death. And Jesus' death is indissolubly linked to His resurrection. Since Easter, dying is no longer what it seems. It is not the end; it is the beginning. It is not a loss; it is the supreme gain. While those without faith try to hide from the inevitability of their death, the Christian can look at it squarely. He does not deny the unpleasant aspects of it; but his faith sees beyond these, because, in Jesus, death has been conquered, surmounted, surpassed and transformed!

In fact, belief in Jesus' resurrection is already a sharing in that resurrection. Through faith in what God did for Jesus, the Son of Man, you and I can experience some of the happiness that Christ felt when He rose from the tomb to that new life of glory. The joy, the confidence we can feel in Jesus' Easter triumph partakes of that very triumph and strengthens our hope that we too will someday enter the fullness of divine light.

Jesus, the Son of God, was at the same time thoroughly human. He knows through His own emotions how we shy away from the very thought of dying and pretend that it happens only to other people.

My soul is troubled now,
yet what should I say —
Father, save me from this hour?

19

But it was for this that I came to this hour.
Father, glorify your name!
(John 12:27, 28)

His desire to reveal the Father's glory (His infinite love for men and His concern for their salvation) enables Jesus to embrace His passion for the sake of far-reaching results that would flow from it.

"Now since the children are men of blood and flesh, Jesus likewise had a full share in ours, that by His death He might rob the devil, the prince of death, of his power, and free those who through fear of death had been slaves their whole life long" (Hebrews 2:14, 15).

The Father is not a God of the dead but of the living. Jesus came that we might have life, and have it abundantly.

I am the resurrection and the life:
whoever believes in me,
though he should die, will come to life;
and whoever is alive and believes in me will never die.
(John 11:25, 26)

To believe in Jesus is to trust Him for everything, even for turning death into richer life. Trust leads to the baptismal commitment, which St. Paul interprets as an immersion in Christ's resurrection:

MYSTERY OF DEATH

Any religious discussion of death must ultimately be concerned with reverence for mystery. From the Christian's point of view, this mystery centers upon the human experience of selfishness and sin as well as upon the person and role of Jesus. Our hope comes from the redemptive strength of Christ's death and resurrection, which is our pledge that what we are and do will not in the end disappear.

Christopher F. Mooney, "Death and the Phenomenon of Life," *America*, April 12, 1975.

"Are you not aware that we who were baptized into Christ Jesus were baptized into His death? Through baptism into His death we were buried with Him, so that, just as Christ was raised from the dead by the glory of the Father, we too might live a new life. If we have been united with Him through likeness to His death, so shall we be through a like resurrection" (Romans 6:3-5).

Plunged into the resurrection — that is a good definition of a Christian. The Jesus we are one with is the Jesus of glory, the Jesus who is the plenitude of being.

WE HAVE NOTHING TO FEAR

Since we have already passed through death, Jesus' death, we have nothing to fear from it now. Life does not end; it changes into a more wonderful form of life, as the caterpillar blossoms into the butterfly. Our personalities, our deepest desires — all that is best in us perdures and finds scope for its highest and complete fulfillment...

No faith is more "solidly established" than faith in the person of Jesus. He Himself is the way, the truth and the life. Part of the reason why many find themselves unequal to the challenges of this confusing time is that the object of their faith is too abstract — limited to theological formulations and principles...

The most dynamic dimension of faith is the personal relationship with Jesus, and through Him with the Father and the Spirit. As this grows, so does love; and perfect love casts out the fear of death.

Eternal life is this:
to know You, the only true God,
and Him whom You have sent, Jesus Christ.
(John 17:3)

Give yourself to Jesus. When, every day, you can say with joy, "Lord Jesus, receive all that I am," you can be sure that you, like Stephen, have already conquered death.

"We cannot rationally feel sorry for the departed person...because as dead he is completely insensible to all such things as any piece of earth or non-living matters. He is just exactly as non-existent as he was before birth and conception."

A Humanist View of Death

Corliss Lamont

Corliss Lamont is a former director of The American Humanist Association. He is the author of many works on humanism, including *The Philosophy of Humanism.* This viewpoint is taken from his book *The Illusion of Immortality.*

Consider the following questions while reading:

1. Why is death neither a reward nor a great evil, according to the author?
2. What is the author's view of life after death?
3. What opinion does the author have of the Christian view of death? Do you agree?

DEATH IS THE END

In justice to death it must be stated that the fate of those who die, whether early or late, is not really very dire. For if we are right in calling immortality an illusion, the dead have no consciousness that they are missing life or that the living are missing them. They cannot grieve over being parted from those whom they love. After life's fitful fever they sleep well; nothing can touch them further, not even dreams. The grave, as Job said, is a place where the wicked cease from troubling and the weary are at rest. Those who have passed on prematurely or in any other way can experience no sting, no sorrow, no disappointment, no remorse, no anything. As Epicurus pithily summed up the matter three hundred years before the birth of Christ: "When we are, death is not; and when death is, we are not." Only if there is a future life need we worry about the dead or need the dead worry about themselves. Only immortality can disturb their eternal peace.

If death is the end, we can feel sorry for ourselves that we have lost a dear friend and for our country or humanity in general that it has lost a man of distinguished abilities; but we cannot rationally feel sorry for the departed person himself, since he is non-existent and can know neither sorrow nor gladness. We cannot be sorry for him as dead, but only for him as dying and as dying unwillingly, conscious that he was leaving this life prematurely with much of his rightful human experience being denied him. We can continue to regret that he as a living person was not able to go on enjoying the goods of existence; we can wish intensely that he were alive again so that he could share our pleasure in this or that. But it is unreasonable to transfer these wishes and regrets to the departed *as dead*, because as dead he is as completely insensible to all such things as any piece of earth or non-living matter. He is just exactly as non-existent as he was before birth and conception...

DEATH AS REWARD OR PUNISHMENT

It is, however, misleading to talk of death as a "reward," since a true reward like a true punishment entails conscious experience of the fact. To him, then, who sacrifices his life for some ideal and goes forever into the blank silences of oblivion, death is hardly a reward. While some men surrender up their lives on behalf of their fellows feeling sure of attaining eternal bliss thereby, there are many others who do so in the full knowledge that death means their absolute end.

No higher type of morality exists than to make one's death count in this fashion. There may come a time in the career of any man when to die will prove more effective for his central purposes than to live; when through his death what he stands for will become more clear and convincing than in any other way. The great unyielding martyrs of the past, men like Socrates and Jesus, have established this point beyond cavil. And many lesser persons — the unnumbered, unsung heroes of history and everyday existence — have likewise demonstrated their contempt for death in the name of life or of love or of some other supreme commitment.

It has usually been assumed that death as such is a very great evil and the worst enemy of man. Now certain specific ways in which death has manifested itself throughout human history, constantly striking down individuals and indeed multitudes in the prime of life and appearing in innumerable ugly forms, are correctly to be classified as evil. Yet death in and

FINITE EXISTENCE?

Man also denies the reality of death by believing in the immortality of his person. This belief can take two different forms. It may take the form of the assumption that the finiteness of man's biological existence is but apparent and that his body will live on in another world. It can also take the form of the assumption that what is specifically human in man will survive the destruction of his body and that man's soul will live on forever, either separated from any body or reincarnated in someone else's. This belief in personal immortality, in defiance of the empirical evidence of the finiteness of man's biological existence, is of course peculiar to the religious realm. It presupposes the existence of a world which is not only inaccessible to the senses but also superior to the world of the senses in that what is truly human in man is there preserved forever.

Hans J. Morgenthau, "Death in the Nuclear Age," from *The Modern Vision of Death*, Nathan A. Scott, Jr., ed.

of itself, as a phenomenon of Nature, is not an evil. There is nothing mysterious about death, nothing supernatural about it, that could legitimately lead to the interpretation that it is a divine punishment inflicted upon men and other living creatures. On the contrary, death is an altogether natural thing and has played a useful and necessary role in the long course of biological evolution. In fact, without this much-maligned institution of death, which has given the fullest and most serious meaning to the survival of the fittest and thus has rendered possible the upward surge of organic species, it is clear that the animal known as man would never have evolved at all...

LIFE IS AFFIRMED BY DEATH

Living and dying, birth and death, are essential and corre-lative aspects of the same biological and evolutionary processes. Life affirms itself *through* death, which during an early era of evolution was brought into existence *by* life and derives its entire significance *from* life. In the dynamic and creative flux of Nature the same living organisms do not go on indefinitely, but retire from the scene at a certain stage and so give way to newborn and lustier vitality...

When we attain the realization that death finishes the story, we know the worst. And that worst is not really very bad. It is, in fact, relatively so far from bad that traditional Christianity and other religions have always insisted that for us sinful humans to escape with mere extinction at the end of our lives would be a terrible violation of justice and would throw grave doubts on the existence of cosmic morality. To understand that death is the necessary and inevitable conclusion of our personal careers enables us to look this fateful event in the face with dignity and calm. Such understanding provides an invaluable stimulus towards that high art of dying which should be an aim of all mature and civilized men.

"Man is immortal: in BODY, through his children; in THOUGHT, through the survival of his memory; in INFLU- ENCE, by virtue of the continuance of his personality as a force among those who come after him; and IDEALLY, through the identification with the timeless things of the spirit."

A Jewish View of Death

Earl A. Grollman

Rabbi Earl A. Grollman is the spiritual leader of the Beth El Temple Center in Belmont, Massachusetts. He is the author of *Explaining Death to Children.*

Consider the following questions while reading:

1. **What does the author mean by the term "the democracy of death"?**
2. **How are people immortal, according to Jewish belief?**

Earl A. Grollman, *Concerning Death: A Practical Guide for the Living.* Re- printed by permission of Beacon Press. Copyright © 1974 by Earl A. Grollman.

THE INEVITABILITY OF DEATH

"The Lord God formed man of dust from the ground, and breathed into his nostrils the breath of life, and man became a living being" (Genesis 2:7). So the Psalmist says that when God sends forth His breath, living beings, whether men or animals, are created, and when God takes His breath away, they die (Psalms 104:29-30). When man's "breath departs, he returns to his earth" (Psalms 146:4).

Death is regarded by Jews as real — quite dreadfully real. It is the completion of life conceived in its concreteness, the rupture of the pleasures of family and friends, the destruction of the possibility of man's enjoying the praise of God. The "wise women" from Tekoa in 2 Samuel 14:14 remark, "We must all die; we are like water spilt on the ground, which cannot be gathered up again." According to Ecclesiastes 9:5, "The dead know nothing." *Sheol* is "the land of gloom and deep darkness, the land of gloom and chaos" (Job 10:21-22) and "the land of primeval ruins" (Ezekiel 26:20); "the land of silence" (Psalms 94:17). "In death there is no remembrance of Thee; in *Sheol* who can give Thee praise?" (Psalms 115:17).

No form of human existence can escape the democracy of death. It is part of the processes of birth, growth, and decay. He knows that "like the grass of the field, he is one whose place will know him no more" (Psalms 103:15). "Man that is born of woman is of few days...he comes forth like a flower, and withers; he flees like a shadow, and continues not...his days are determined, and the number of his months is with Thee, and Thou has appointed his bounds that he cannot pass" (Job 14:1-5).

In Judaism, death is both real and inescapable. A person should know that he must die, for death is an organic, natural, and logical part of life. For what man can live and never see death?

THE DEATHLESSNESS OF MAN'S SPIRIT

With the development of the beliefs of other religions in retribution and resurrection, Judaism turned its attention to what happens after death. Whatever one's belief in a world to come, there is the acceptance that man transcends death in naturalistic fashion. Man is immortal; in *body,* through his children; in *thought,* through the survival of his memory; in *influence,* by virtue of the continuance of his personality

27

as a force among those who come after him; and *ideally*, through the identification with the timeless things of the spirit.

A commentator of the Bible explained this immortality of influence in a discussion of "And Jacob lived" (Genesis 47:28). Of how few individuals can we repeat a phrase like, "And Jacob lived"? When many people die, a death notice appears in the press. In reality it is a life notice because, but for it, the world would never have known the person had ever been alive. Only he who has been a force for human goodness, and abides in hearts and in a world made better by his presence, can be said to have *lived*. Only such a one is heir to immortality.

THE GOOD LIVE ON

Only he who has been a force for human goodness, and abides in hearts and in a world made better by his presence, can be said to have lived. *Only such a one is heir to immortality.*

Death is not the end of life — not just in terms of another possible world, but in the real and tangible sense of ongoing ideals and influence that continue shaping the affections one has held and served. Life points always to the future, when one shall become another heritage and influence, whether in ordinary personal memory, or through the thoughts and acts and decisions that give a lasting grace to ongoing human existence. The ancient Egyptians buried their dead with all the things a person needs, such as clothes, weapons, and food, and were more preoccupied with death than with life; the Hebrews, on the other hand, believed that in the hour of man's departure from this world, neither silver nor gold nor precious stones nor pearls accompany him, but only study and good works.

"To meet death, not only as an event at the end of life but as an ever-present ingredient in the life-process itself, is the final goal to be sought in both Hinduism and Buddhism."

A Hindu–Buddhist View of Death

J. Bruce Long

J. Bruce Long is an educator, minister and fundamentalist Christian. Born in Elk City, Oklahoma, he graduated from the Arizona Bible Institute in 1958. Currently, he is treasurer of the Arizona Regional Independent Fundamental Church of America.

Consider the following questions while reading:

1. What does the author claim is the final goal to be sought in both Hinduism and Buddhism?
2. What does the author mean when he states "in every instant we are born; in every instant we die"?
3. What differences do you see between the Eastern (Hindu-Buddhist) and Western (Judeo-Christian) views of death? What similarities?

J. Bruce Long, "The Death That Ends Death In Hinduism and Buddism." From Elisabeth Kubler-Ross, *Death: The Final Stage of Growth.* Englewood Cliffs: Prentice-Hall, 1975.

THE FINAL GOAL

There is general agreement between Hinduism and Buddhism that no human life can be filled with a sense of meaning and efficacious action unless it is lived in full acceptance of the fact of death. He who tries to ignore death by deluding himself into believing that he, his relatives, and his possessions will endure forever, robs himself of the purposeful life which can come only to him who unflinchingly accepts death as an integral part of life. On the other hand, that person who faces death calmly, courageously, and confidently—desiring neither to flee it nor to rush into its grasp—will come to recognize death not as an enemy or a robber but as an ever-present companion and ultimately, as a friend. To meet death, not only as an event at the end of life but as an ever-present ingredient in the life-process itself, is the final goal to be sought in both Hinduism and Buddhism.

Buddhist doctrine defines death as a cutting off of the life-force or a total nonfunctioning of the physical body and the mind. Not that the life-force is totally destroyed with the death of the body; it is merely displaced and transformed to continue functioning in another form. Every birth is, in fact, a rebirth. Many Buddhists believe that rebirth occurs immediately after death. Others believe that forty-nine days separate death and rebirth in an "intermediary state" (*Bardo*), graphically described in the *Tibetan Book of the Dead*, about which we will speak in greater detail presently.

NO BEGINNING OR END

Birth and death, when viewed at the cosmic level of perception, describes the outer limits of the life of both the individual person and of the cosmos. Strictly speaking, neither human beings nor the universe itself experiences either an absolute beginning or an absolute end. When this same drama of birth and death is viewed as the microlevel in terms of seconds and fractions of seconds rather than years or aeons, birth and death are discovered to occur almost simultaneously in each instant of time. The human person is nothing more than a conglomeration of "aggregates" (i.e. body, sensations, perceptions, mental formations, and consciousness) which, taken together form the mind-body organism engaged in the process of coming-to-being and passing-away in every moment.

But, according to Buddhist teachings, there is no single permanent, unchanging entity or substance constituting the

Self or Soul which endures in a uniform state from moment to moment and from lifetime to lifetime. That phenomenon which we customarily call "the self" in speaking of "I myself" or "you yourself" is nothing more than a continuity of a series of psycho-physiological occasions (described by the American psychologist, William James, as "the stream of consciousness") which undergoes an unbroken series of alterations in every moment. As one teacher states it: "When the Aggregates arise, decay and die, O monk, every moment you are born, decay and die." Thus, in every instant we are born; in every instant we die. Birth and death are two almost indistinguishable and imperceptible strands of a single rope of existence.

LIFE: FROM BIRTH TO BIRTH

When a philosophy regards personality as extending beyond life and death, it treats the subject of death more earnestly and positively. When the contrary view is taken, namely that death puts an end to life and personality since these belong only to waking consciousness, then death becomes an issue to be generally evaded, however inevitable an evil it is. Nevertheless, and particularly in the East, the idea of one's self as traversing and transcending the three states of wakefulness, dream, and deep sleep has taken shape through various forms and stages in the history of man's self-reflection. Accordingly, what we call death took on the significance and appeal of changing old clothes for new and better ones and the meaning of physical death became that of a moment in the unending process of life. Thus the word "life" is not restricted in its meaning to the span of the life of man between birth and death. Life is a process; there is no process without change, no change without becoming, and no becoming without the intervening moments of discarding dispensable elements of the life-process. Death is one such moment.

This typically Indian view is shared by Hindus, Buddhists, and Jains alike. Life is an unending drive from birth to birth. Yet it is not the same as immortality. It is within the realm of mortality, change, and becoming.

P. T. Raju, *Death and Eastern Thought*

The human self, therefore, is composed of a stream of consciousness, changing momentarily and filled with impressions and tendencies created by good and evil actions (*karma*) which at death is transposed to a new mode of being, while the imagined "self" who thinks in terms of "I" and "mine" does not survive from one moment to the next and hence, does not transmigrate.

The Buddhists, like the Hindus, believe that there are differences in the quality of deaths, just as there are differences in the quality of births and existences. The differences in deaths depend upon the difference between disciplined and undisciplined living, between pure and impure mind or between "carefulness" and "carelessness." "Carefulness is the path of the deathless; carelessness is the path to death... The constantly meditative, the ever earnestly striving ones, realize the bond-free, supreme Nirvana" (*Dhammapada 21-23*).

The "soul" or "the fruits of the karma" of a deceased person who is still trapped by the bonds of "desire," according to popular Buddhist belief, will go immediately after death to Yama's judgment chamber where, after a waiting period of seven days, he is required to cross a treacherous river with three current speeds simultaneously (representing three karmic destinies of hell: human beings, animals and hungry ghosts). Those who cross the river successfully are ushered into a Paradise or a Happy Land, ruled by Amitabha ("Boundless Light") who will provide a rebirth in his Paradise for those who have true faith in him and praise his holy name...

The message of the Buddha to all suffering humanity is this: everything inevitably comes to extinction even though it may last for a millennium. Everything must be parted from what it desires in the end. Recognize that all living things (mineral, vegetable, animal, human, and divine) are subject to the law of death. Therefore, recognize the true nature of the living world and do not be anxious about your life or your death. "When the light of true knowledge has dispelled the darkness of ignorance, when all existence has been seen as without substance, peace ensues when life draws to an end, which seems to cure a long illness at last. Everything, whether stationary or movable is bound to perish in the end. Be ye therefore mindful and vigilant." (*Buddhacarita* XXVI 88 *ff.*)

"Death is the final stage of growth in this life. There is no total death. Only the body dies. The self or spirit, or whatever you may wish to label it, is eternal."

Death is the Final Stage of Growth

Elisabeth Kubler–Ross

Dr. Elisabeth Kubler-Ross, a leading authority on death, is the author of *On Death and Dying*, *Questions and Answers on Death and Dying*, *To Live Until We Say Goodby*, and *Death: The Final Stage of Growth*, from which this viewpoint is taken. She is founder/director of Shanti Nilaya, a healing center in Escondido, California. She holds nineteen honorary doctoral degrees, and serves on the boards of directors and advisory boards of many hospices and healing centers throughout the world.

Consider the following questions while reading:
1. **Why does the author think death is the key to life?**
2. **Why does she claim death is the final stage of growth?**
3. **Do you think various church leaders would agree with this viewpoint? Do you agree?**

Elisabeth Kubler-Ross, *Death: The Final Stage of Growth*. Englewood Cliffs: Prentice-Hall, 1975. Reprinted with permission from the author.

DEATH IS THE KEY TO LIFE

There is no need to be afraid of death. It is not the end of the physical body that should worry us. Rather, our concern must be to *live* while we're alive—to release our inner selves from the spiritual death that comes with living behind a façade designed to conform to external definitions of who and what we are. Every individual human being born on this earth has the capacity to become a unique and special person unlike any who has ever existed before or will ever exist again. But to the extent that we become captives of culturally defined role expectations and behaviors—stereotypes, not ourselves,— we block our capacity for self-actualization. We interfere with our becoming all that we can be.

Death is the key to the door of life. It is through accepting the finiteness of our individual existences that we are enabled to find the strength and courage to reject those extrinsic roles and expectations and to devote each day of our lives—however long they may be—to growing as fully as we are able. We must learn to draw on our inner resources, to define ourselves in terms of the feedback we receive from our own internal valuing system rather than trying to fit ourselves into some illfitting stereotyped role.

It is the denial of death that is partially responsible for people living empty, purposeless lives; for when you live as if you'll live forever, it becomes too easy to postpone the things you know that you must do. You live your life in preparation for tomorrow or in remembrance of yesterday, and meanwhile, each today is lost. In contrast, when you fully understand that each day you awaken could be the last you have, you take the time *that day* to grow, to become more of who you really are, to reach out to other human beings....

There is an urgency that each of you, no matter how many days or weeks or months or years you have to live, commit yourself to growth. We are living in a time of uncertainty, anxiety, fear, and despair. It is essential that you become aware of the light, power, and strength within each of you, and that you learn to use those inner resources in service of your own and others' growth...

Humankind will survive only through the commitment and involvement of individuals in their own and others' growth and development as human beings. This means development of loving and caring relationships in which all members are as committed to the growth and happiness of the others as they are to their own. Through commitment to personal growth individual human beings will also make their contribution to the growth and development—the evolution—of the whole species to become all that humankind can and is meant to be. Death is the key to that evolution. For only when we understand the real meaning of death to human existence will we have the courage to become what we are destined to be...

Elisabeth Kubler-Ross

OUR LIMITED TIME

It is all within you if you look and are not afraid. Death can show us the way, for when we know and understand completely that our time on this earth is limited, and that we have no way of knowing when it will be over, then we must live each day as if it were the only one we had.

THE SELF IS ETERNAL

Death is the final stage of growth in this life. There is no total death. Only the body dies. The self or spirit, or whatever you may wish to label it, is eternal. You may interpret this in any way that makes you comfortable.

If you wish, you may view the eternal essence of your exist- ence in terms of the impact your every mood and action has on those you touch, and then in turn, on those they touch, and on and on—even long after your life span is completed. You will never know, for example, the rippling effects of the smile and words of encouragement you give to other human beings with whom you come in contact.

You may be more comfortable and comforted by a faith that there is a source of goodness, light, and strength greater than any of us individually, yet still within us all, and that each essential self has an existence that transcends the finiteness of the physical and contributes to that greater power.

Death, in this context, may be viewed as the curtain be- tween the existence that we are conscious of and one that is hidden from us until we raise that curtain. Whether we open it symbolically in order to understand the finiteness of the ex- istence we know, thus learning to live each day the best we can, or whether we open it in actuality when we end that physical existence is not the issue. What is important is to realize that whether we understand fully why we are here or what will happen when we die, it is our purpose as human beings to grow—to look within ourselves to find and build upon that source of peace and understanding and strength which is our inner selves, and to reach out to others with love, acceptance, patient guidance, and hope for what we all may become together.*

*A cassette recording, "Elisabeth Kubler-Ross Talks to High School Students," is available through Shanti Nilaya, P.O. Box 2396, Escondido, CA 92025.

WRITE YOUR OWN EPITAPH

An epitaph is a brief statement (often found on a tombstone) in remembrance of a dead person. It usually tries to express in a few words what was significant or memorable about the person's life.

Note the epitaphs of three famous individuals on the following page.

Instructions

STEP 1

In a sentence or two, write your own epitaph. (Remember, your epitaph is how you want to be remembered. If someone were to read your tombstone a hundred years from now, this is all they would know about you.)

STEP 2

Write an epitaph for each of the following:
1. A relative or friend who is dead.
2. A public figure who is dead. (You may use a government official, an actor, an athlete, etc.)

STEP 3

Select a classmate who you know well and who knows you well. Each of you write an epitaph for the other.

37

"Write on my gravestone, 'Infidel, Traitor' — infidel to every church that compromises with the strong; traitor to every government that oppresses the people."

Wendell Phillips, 1811-1884; famous American orator and abolitionist.

"In presenting this scroll, I am rewarding 'a good public servant.' I hope that will be my epitaph."

Harry S. Truman; spoken at an awards ceremony on September 7, 1945.

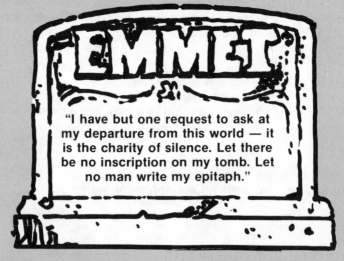

EMMET

"I have but one request to ask at my departure from this world — it is the charity of silence. Let there be no inscription on my tomb. Let no man write my epitaph."

Robert Emmet, Irish nationalist; spoken as he was about to be hung by the British in 1803.

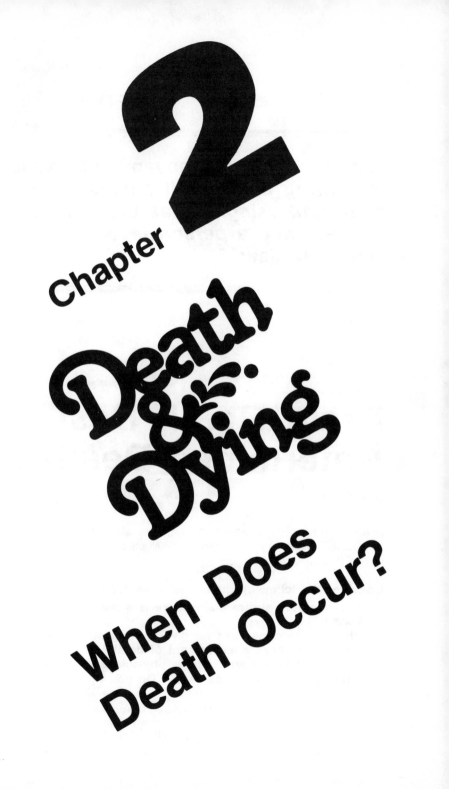

Chapter

2

Death & Dying

When Does Death Occur?

"There is a current movement towards measuring death as it occurs in the brain and using this as the criterion for declaring a person legally and medically dead."

Brain Death Best Determines Death

Brad R. Reynolds

Brad R. Reynolds, a Jesuit priest, was studying at Weston School of Theology in Cambridge, Massachusetts, when he wrote this statement.

Consider the following questions while reading:
1. Why does the author claim there is a need to redefine death?
2. What two reasons does he give in suggesting that brain death is the best measurement of death?
3. What role does the author think physicians should have in determining the point of death? Do you agree?

Brad R. Reynolds, "The Eerie Need to Redefine Death", *America*, September 27, 1975. Reprinted with permission of America Press, Inc., 106 West 56th Street, New York, N.Y. 10019. © 1975 All rights reserved.

While advances in medical science over the last half-century have proven near-miraculous for the living, they have put the dead and dying in a precarious position. The advances in organ transplantation and inventions of mechanical ways to resuscitate, recycle and revive have provided countless persons with new life when previously their illnesses would have been declared hopeless. But for the dead and dying, these same advances and inventions raise formidable questions concerning not only their right to use the medical aids available, but even questions concerning their rights to their own organs.

THE NEED TO REDEFINE DEATH

A most pressing issue for both the living and dying is the redefining of, or establishing the criteria for, death. In earlier and "less advanced" times, death was not difficult to determine. If the person was not breathing and there was no detectable heartbeat, he was dead. There were, at times, mistakes. Ghoulish tales of clawed coffin lids and elaborate alarm systems buried with the supposed-dead provide adequate record of such mistakes. For years, the methods of determining death remained the same, relying upon physical and observable characteristics. Dr. William Poe's book *The Old Person in Your Home*, provides as adequate a listing of the characteristics as any: "The eyes become fixed, with opened pupils which do not respond to light, the heartbeat and breathing cease. The mouth may be open and motionless. The skin turns pale and cold. The skin in contact with the bed may become bluish or purple—livor mortis. After thirty to sixty minutes the limp extremities may become stiff—rigor mortis."

Legally, the definition of death lists the cessation of respiratory and circulatory functions as the two main criteria. *Black's Law Dictionary* has defined death as "the cessation of life; the ceasing to exist; defined by physicians as a total stoppage of the circulation of the blood, and a cessation of the animal and vital functions consequent thereon, such as respiration, pulsation, etc."

But now the old medical and legal definitions are outmoded and, in fact, dangerous. They are getting more so every day, with new advancement in medicine.

"I remember when cessation of heartbeat was an observation on which we simply pronounced the patient as dead;

41

now, this is a medical syndrome known as cardiac arrest," reports Dr. William P. Williamson of the University of Kansas in the *Journal of the American Medical Association.* "Cessation of respiration is a symptom also formerly implying death, which can now be corrected by an ingenious and devilishly efficient machine known as a mechanical respirator."...

The medical and legal professions have often clashed over their understandings of death. One court decision claimed that: "Death is not a continuing event and is an event that takes place at a precise time." But Dr. Pierre H. Muller took issue with the law in the *World Medical Journal.* "Death is a process and not a moment in time, as the law believes. During the process there are a series of physical and chemical changes, starting before the medicolegal times of death and continuing afterward."

BOLD AND INNOVATIVE

By permitting their physicians to use the concept of brain death, the people of Kansas have scored a legislative precedent. Nowhere else in the common-law world do doctors have knowledge of this right prospectively, and in this age of medicolegal uncertainty, this statute stands as quite an accomplishment.

Don Harper Mills, "The Kansas Death Statute: Bold and Innovative," *The New England Journal of Medicine,* 1971.

And today, because of the successful and increasing use of organ transplants, the medical and legal professions are even more in need of a common understanding of death. Physicians, in need of a heart for a patient, find themselves unable to remove the organ from a man whose brain may have died and yet whose heart continues to pump. The court, as the protector of an individual's rights, is cautious, lest an over-anxious doctor, in his haste to save one life, quickens the death of another. And both sides face the same dilemmas in regard to mechanical life-supporting devices. The question of when to "pull the plug" on machines such as artificial respirators and declare the patient dead has become almost hopelessly fouled in the legal, medical and moral ramifications of such an act.

BRAIN DEATH

Because of these mounting difficulties, and through recent efforts to understand death better, there is a current movement towards measuring death as it occurs in the brain and using this as the criterion for declaring a person legally and medically dead. The brain as the center for all impulses and cognition, is now recognized as the center for life forces. The functions of the brain separate man from all other species. It is the harbor of reason, memory, flights of fantasy and the intangible spirit of man.

The advantages of defining brain death over respiratory or circulatory cessation are twofold. 1) If the life functions are being maintained by artificial means, activity can be maintained indefinitely, without regard to conscious life, the psychological effect upon family and friends and cost. Death of the brain becomes a point of determination, past which other life functions are meaningless for that individual. 2) Brain death often occurs prior to the cessation of other bodily functions, facilitating the use of organs in transplant operations...

For physicians and scientists, the movement towards defining brain death has proved beneficial from a purely medical or scientific standpoint. But legally they are in trouble. Most states still abide by the old understanding of death as defined in *Black's Law Dictionary*. Consequently, a physician or surgeon who turns off life–supportive machinery or transplants vital organs before "heart death" has taken place, can theoretically be held liable for homicide, even if "brain death" has obviously occurred. But the laws are slowly being changed...

Few would disagree that death should rightfully be determined by the physicians. But to the extent that the determination includes legal and moral considerations, lawyers and ethicians must enter into the picture. As soon as an issue involves the rights to life and death, then the matter extends beyond just the medical profession. So, while doctors and scientists continue both refining and defining the process of death, the legal and moral involvements of the patient must concomitantly be kept in focus...

The moral and ethical implications are watchdogged by many: the medical profession itself, the legal profession, the churches and professional ethicians have all contributed to facing and dealing with the difficult moral issues that have arisen. While there is little danger that the medical profession will turn into an organization of Frankensteins, idling around morgues and accident-prone road intersections, there is still the question of how far into the dying process a surgeon must wait before he can declare a person dead and still hope to save some of the living tissue or organs for transplanting. And when do ordinary life-supporting means end and the extraordinary begin? How long can a person continue to live if his respiration and circulation are maintained by artificial means, and still remain a person, before he becomes merely a biological organism maintained by mechanical means?...

Efforts to connect the event of death to a certain point along the process of dying will continue for quite some time. There will continue to be small steps forward, such as the Harvard ad hoc committee's criteria for brain death, and flying leaps, such as the neocortex death proposal. Throughout the search it will become increasingly important for scientists, physicians, lawyers and ethicians to work in close harmony with one another. Physicians must retain the right to declare the point of death, but only after considering the rights of the individuals and the moral principles involved.

"Everyone can tell when a person is definitely dead. But all the expertise in the world cannot tell when a person is still possibly alive...and to allow the doing of certain things to a person on the basis of a legal definition linked to brain activity would, therefore be tactically disastrous."

The Brain Death Trap

Frank Morriss

An attorney (graduate of Georgetown University School of Law, 1948) and former news editor of the Denver Catholic Register and the National Register, Frank Morriss is currently a freelance writer and contributing editor to *The Wanderer*. A prolific writer, his numerous publications include *Boy of Philadelphia, Saints for the Small, The Conservative Imperative* and *The Catholic as Citizen*. He resides in Wheat Ridge, Colorado.

Consider the following questions while reading:

1. How does the author see the use of brain death as a criteria for death as a threat to the pro-life side of the abortion issue?
2. What does he suggest be used to determine death instead of brain death?
3. What does the author mean when he says that "human life is a unity"? Do you agree?

Frank Morriss, "The 'Brain Death' Trap", *The Wanderer*, February 15, 1979. Reprinted with permission of the author and publisher.

Acquiescing in the idea of "brain death"—particularly a statutory definition—would be tactically disastrous for the pro-life movement. The fundamental reason is that the child in its earliest hours of conception certainly does not have brain or brain stem as such, and theoretically might fit under a "brain death" definition. But the child is a live unity, the unifying agent being the human soul.

We can only say for certain that death is present when dissolution takes place. Everyone can tell when a person is definitely dead. It takes no medical expertise. But all the expertise in the world cannot tell when a person is still possibly alive, in the absence of dissolution. And to allow the doing of certain things to a person on the basis of a legal definition linked to brain activity would, therefore, be tactically disastrous.

Does a child become alive only when brain and brain stem are present, and brain activity can be registered? If we answer yes, we have obviously thrown away our fundamental argument against abortion from conception on. If we say no, then we can hardly agree that similar criteria should be established for declaring a person already born to be dead.

I understand that mere cellular nervous "life" can be kept going practically indefinitely without a brain, even in a body severed from a head. But we should not fall for the argument, "Well, would you call that human life?"

What we must do is allow traditional determination of life to prevail. That sufficed civilization for hundreds and thousands of years. Why the desire to change now? Some will say because of technical advances in keeping life going artifi-

---

A DANGEROUS MOVE

The claim that death occurs when the brain dies is opinion to be sure, but it is not, and by the very nature of the case cannot be, medical opinion. To leave such decision-making in the hands of scientifically trained professionals is a dangerous move.

Robert M. Veatch, "Brain Death," Institute of Society, Ethics and the Life Sciences.

---

cially. But that evades the heart of the issue—should we allow the state to fix death at a point where the common experience of mankind could not say for certain whether or not the soul is present in the body? The only good answer from a pro-life position is "no."

Actually, we can only speculate as to whether death occurs when the matter is no longer suitable for being "informed" by the soul, or whether a departure of the soul brings about the unsuitability for life of a body.

The whole grisly discussion of severed heads and bodies smacks too much of some idea of a divisibility of human life, and does not match the Thomistic idea that equates the presence of a spirit with human life. Why indeed is a living brain the seat of the soul more than a living toe? In Thomistic philosophy the problem is not an intelligent one. Human life is a unity—either there is mere cellular growth and activity present, and the body is therefore dead; or the soul is present and the person is alive.

We should also separate definition of death from the moral problem of keeping a person alive by extraordinary means. If a person is legally declared dead, and we accept that as a moral determinant, then we need do nothing for that entity at all—ordinary or extraordinary, other than give it a decent burial. Theoretically, we would not have to wait for a heart to stop beating, or lungs to stop breathing to bury something

---

AMA OPPOSITION

While some doctors favor brain death legislation, the American Medical Association is on record as opposing it, calling such laws "neither desirable nor necessary." Medical experts have also pointed out that cessation of total brain function cannot be measured infallibly. They maintain it should continue to be used in conjunction with heart and lung stoppage, which can be accurately observed, at least until there is consensus on how it is to be determined.

Mary Koster, Vice President, Minnesota Citizens Concerned for Life, from a column appearing in the *Minneapolis Star*.

---

that is truly "dead," or to remove his or her organs. In other words, isn't there something very artificial about accepting a definition of death dependent simply upon brain activity?

The moral question of "pulling the plug" involves persons truly alive, and our duties toward such a person. Brain death definitions have far deeper implications, and should not be accepted simply to solve difficulties that should be decided on a different level.

"Life is certainly not an all–or–none phenomenon. Clearly the amount of living matter follows a long trajectory of growth and decline with no very clear beginning and a notably indeterminate end."

Death is a Process

Robert S. Morison

Robert S. Morison is professor of science and society, Cornell University, and a member of the task force on death and dying of the Institute of Society, Ethics and the Life Sciences.

Consider the following questions while reading:

1. What point does the author try to make with the statement, "life may reach a state where there is no longer an ethical imperative to preserve it"?
2. What observation does the author make about when life begins?
3. When does he think life ends?

Robert S. Morison, "Death: Process or Event?", *Science*, Vol. 173, pp. 694-698, August 20, 1971. Copyright © 1971 by the American Association for the Advancement of Science. Reprinted with permission of the author and publisher.

Most discussions of death and dying shift uneasily, and often more or less unconsciously, from one point of view to another. On the one hand, the common noun "death" is thought of as standing for a clearly defined event, a step function that puts a sharp end to life. On the other hand, dying is seen as a long-drawn-out process that begins when life itself begins and is not completed in any given organism until the last cell ceases to convert energy.

The first view is certainly the more traditional one. Indeed, it is so deeply embedded, not only in literature and art, but also in the law, that it is hard to free ourselves from it and from various associated attitudes that greatly influence our behavior...

IS A "REDEFINITION" OF DEATH ENOUGH?

Fewer and fewer people die quietly in their beds while relatives and friends live on, unable to stay the inevitable course. More and more patients are subject to long, continued intervention; antibiotics, intravenous feeding, artificial respiration, and even artificially induced heartbeats sustain an increasingly fictional existence. All this costs money—so much money, in fact, that the retirement income of a surviving spouse may disappear in a few months. There are other costs, less tangible but perhaps more important—for example, the diversion of scarce medical resources from younger people temporarily threatened by acute but potentially curable illnesses. Worst of all is the strain upon a family that may have to live for years in close association with a mute, but apparently living, corpse.

DO WE KNOW?

We do not know with certainty the borderline between life and death, and a definition cannot substitute for knowledge. Moreover, we have sufficient grounds for suspecting that the artificially supported condition of the comatose patient may still be one of life, however reduced—i.e., for doubting that, even with the brain function gone, he is completely dead. In this state of marginal ignorance and doubt the only course to take is to lean over backward toward the side of possible life.

Hans Jonas, *Philosophical Essays: From Ancient Creed to Technological Man.*

An even more disturbing parameter has recently been added to the equation. It appears that parts of the dying body may acquire values greater than the whole. A heart, a kidney, someday even a lung or a liver, can mean all of life for some much younger, more potentially vigorous and happy "donee."

Indeed, it appears that it is primarily this latter set of facts which has led to recent proposals for redefining death. The most prominent proposals place more emphasis on the information-processing capacity of the brain and rather less on the purely mechanical and metabolic activities of the body as a whole than do the present practices. The great practical merit of these proposals is that they place the moment of death somewhat earlier in the continuum of life than the earlier definition did. By so doing, they make it easier for the physician to disoontinue therapy while some of what used to be considered "signs of life" are still present, thus sparing relatives, friends, and professional attendants the anguish and the effort of caring for a "person" who has lost most of the attributes of personality. Furthermore, parts of the body which survive death, as newly defined, may be put to other, presumably more important uses, since procedures such as autopsies or removal of organs can be undertaken without being regarded as assaults...

DEATH IS A PROCESS

As our skill in simulating the physiological processes underlying life continues to increase in disproportion to our capacity to maintain its psychological, emotional, or spiritual quality, the difficulty of regarding death as a single, more or less coherent event, resulting in the instantaneous dissolution of the organism as a whole, is likely to become more and more apparent. It may not be premature, therefore, to anticipate some of the questions that will then increasingly press upon us. Some of the consequences of adopting the attitude that death is part of a continuous process that is coextensive (almost) with living may be tentatively outlined as follows.

An unprejudiced look at the biological facts suggests, indeed, that the "life" of a complex vertebrate like man is not a clearly defined entity with sharp discontinuities at both ends. On the contrary, the living human being starts inconspicuously, unconsciously, and at an unknown time, with the conjugation of two haploid cells. In a matter of some hours, this new cell begins to divide. The net number of living cells in the organism continues to increase for perhaps 20 years, then begins slowly to decrease. Looked at in this way, life is certainly not an all-or-none phenomenon. Clearly the amount of living matter follows a long trajectory of growth and decline with no very clear beginning and a notably indeterminate end. A similar trajectory can be traced for total energy turnover.

A human life is, of course, far more than a metabolizing mass of organic matter, slavishly obeying the laws of conservation of mass and energy. Particularly interesting are the complex interactions among the individual cells and between the totality and the environment. It is, in fact, this complexity of interaction that gives rise to the concept of human personality or soul.

WHEN IS DEATH?

We now know death is not so much a moment as a process. Medical instruments can keep track of such physical developments, and therein lies a problem: When does death officially occur?

Brad R. Reynolds, "The Eerie Need to Redefine Death," *America*, September 27, 1975.

Whatever metaphors are used to describe the situation, it is clear that it is the complex interactions that make the characteristic human being. The appropriate integration of these interactions is only loosely coupled to the physiological functions of circulation and respiration. The latter continue for a long time after the integrated "personality" has disappeared. Conversely, the natural rhythms of heart and respiration can fail, while the personality remains intact. The complex human organism does not often fail as a unit. The nervous system is, of course, more closely coupled to personality than are the heart and lungs (a fact that is utilized in developing the new definitions of death), but there is clearly something arbitrary in tying the sanctity of life to our ability to detect the electrical potential charges that managed to traverse the impedance of the skull.

If there is no infallible physiological index to what we value about human personality, are we not ultimately forced to make judgments about the intactness and value of the complex interactions themselves?

"There is no need to abandon the traditional understanding of the concept of death: death is the transition from the state of being alive to the state of being dead."

Death is an Event

Leon R. Kass

Dr. Kass is executive secretary of the Committee on the Life Sciences and Social Policy of the National Research Council, National Academy of Sciences. He is also a member of the task force on death and dying of the Institute of Society, Ethics and the Life Sciences.

Consider the following questions while reading:

1. On what point does the author agree with the previous viewpoint?
2. How does the author distinguish between aging and dying?
3. What does the author mean when he says that "the real source of our confusion about death is probably our confusion about living things"?
4. What conclusion does the author come to? Do you agree?

Leon R. Kass, "Death as an Event: A Commentary on Robert Morison", *Science*, Vol. 173, pp. 698-700, August 20, 1971. Copyright © 1971 by the American Association for the Advancement of Science. Reprinted with permission of the publisher.

As I understand R. S. Morison's argument, it consists of these parts, although presented in different order. First: He notes that we face serious practical problems as a result of our unswerving adherence to the principle, "always prolong life." Second: Although *some* of these problems could be solved by updating the "definition of death," such revisions are scientifically and philosophically unsound. Third: The reason for this is that life and death are part of a continuum; it will prove impossible, in practice, to identify any border between them because theory tells us that no such border exists. Thus: We need to abandon both the idea of death as a concrete event and the search for its definition; instead, we must face the fact that our practical problems can only be solved by difficult judgments, based upon a complex cost–benefit analysis, concerning the value of the lives that might or might not be prolonged.

I am in agreement with Morison only on the first point. I think he leads us into philosophical, scientific, moral, and political error. Let me try to show how.

SOME BASIC DISTINCTIONS

The difficulties begin in Morison's beginning, in his failure to distinguish clearly among aging, dying, and dead. His statement that "dying is seen as a long–drawn–out process that begins when life itself begins" would be remarkable, if true, since it would render dying synonymous with living. One consequence would be that murder could be considered merely a farsighted form of euthanasia, a gift to the dying of an early exit from their miseries. But we need not ponder these riddles, because what Morison has done is to confuse dying with aging. Aging (or senescence) apparently does begin early in life (though probably not at conception), but there is no clear evidence that it is ever the cause of death...

As distinguished from aging, dying would be the process leading from the incidence of the "accidental" cause of death to and beyond some border, however ill–defined, after which the organism (or its body) may be said to be dead...

If there is a natural distinction between living and nonliving things, what is the proper way of stating the nature of that difference? What is the real difference between something alive and that "same" something dead? To this crucial question, I shall return later. For the present, it is sufficient to point out that the real source of our confusion about death is probably our confusion about living things. The death of an organism is not understandable because its "aliveness" is not understood except in terms of nonliving matter and motion...

AN ARBITRARY
DECISION

A strictly formal definition of death might be the following:

Death means a complete change in the status of any living entity characterized by the irreversible loss of those characteristics that are essentially significant to it.

Such a definition would apply equally well to a human being, a nonhuman animal, a plant, an organ, a cell, or even metaphorically to a social phenomenon like a society or to any temporally limited entity like a research project, a sports event, or a language. To define the death of a human being, we must recognize the characteristics that are essential to humanness. It is quite inadequate to limit the discussion to the death of the heart or the brain.

Henry Beecher, the distinguished physician who chaired the Harvard committee that proposed a "definition of irreversible coma," has said that "at whatever level we choose..., it is an arbitrary decision" [italics added]. But he goes on, "It is best to choose a level where although the brain is dead, usefulness of other organs is still present" [italics added]. Now, clearly he is not making an "arbitrary decision" any longer. He recognizes that there are policy payoffs. He, like the rest of us, realizes that death already has a well-established meaning...We use the term death to mean the loss of what is essentially significant to an entity — in the case of man, the loss of humanness. The direct link of a word death to what is "essentially significant" means that the task of defining it in this sense is first and foremost a philosophical, theological, ethical task.

Robert M. Veatch, *Death, Dying, and the Biological Revolution.*

THE CONCEPT OF DEATH

There is no need to abandon the traditional understanding of the concept of death: Death is the transition from the state of being alive to the state of being dead. Rather than emphasize the opposition between death and life, an opposition that invites Morison to see the evils wrought by personification, we should concentrate, for our purposes, on the opposition between death and birth (or conception). Both are transitions, however fraught with ambiguities. Notice that the notion of transition leaves open the question of whether the change is abrupt or gradual and whether it is continuous or discontinuous. But these questions about *when* and *how* cannot be adequately discussed without some substantive understanding of *what* it is that dies.

What dies is the organism as a whole. It is this death, the death of the individual human being, that is important for physicians and for the community, not the "death" of organs or cells, which are mere parts...

Death was once recognizable by any ordinary observer who could see (or feel or hear). Today, in some difficult cases, we require further technological manipulation (from testing of reflexes to the electroencephalogram) to make manifest latent signs of a phenomenon, the visible signs of which an earlier intervention has obscured.

In the light of these remarks, I would argue that we should not take our bearings from the small number of unusual cases in which there is doubt. In most cases, there is no doubt. There is no real need to blur the distinction between a man alive and a man dead or to undermine the concept of death as an event. Rather, we should ask, in the light of our traditional concepts (though not necessarily with traditional criteria), whether the persons in the twilight zone are alive or not, and find criteria on the far side of the twilight zone in order to remove any suspicion that a man may be pronounced dead while he is yet alive.

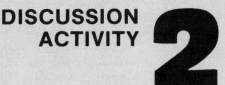

DISTINGUISHING BETWEEN FACT AND OPINION

This discussion exercise is designed to promote experimentation with one's ability to distinguish between fact and opinion. It is a fact, for example, that the United States was militarily involved in the Vietnam War. But to say this involvement served the interests of world peace is an opinion or conclusion. Future historians will agree that American soldiers fought in Vietnam, but their interpretations about the causes and consequences of the war will probably vary greatly.

PART I

Instructions

Consider each of the following statements carefully. Mark O for any statement you feel is an opinion or interpretation of the facts. Mark F for any statement you believe is a fact. Then discuss and compare your judgments with those of other class members.

O = OPINION
F = FACT

_____ 1. A person with a terminal illness should be allowed to die without extraordinary life-preserving measures.

_____ 2. Grief is usually a normal reaction to death.

_____ 3. Hell is a real place.

_____ 4. Funerals are a rip-off.

_____ 5. Death occurs when the brain stops functioning.

_____ 6. The soul lives on after death.

_____ 7. Burial is a more common way of disposing of corpses than cremation.

_____ 8. A dying person often denies that he or she is going to die.

_____ 9. When a Christian dies, he or she is going either to heaven or to hell.

_____ 10. When a humanist dies, he or she is going either to heaven or to hell.

_____ 11. No one can be absolutely certain about the possibilities of life after death.

_____ 12. In general, most religions provide their believers with hope for an afterlife.

_____ 13. An atheist does not believe that there is a life after death.

PART II

Instructions

STEP 1

The class should break into groups of four to six students.

STEP 2

Each small group should try to locate two statements of fact and two statements of opinion in the book.

STEP 3

Each group should choose a student to record its statements.

STEP 4

The class should discuss and compare the small groups' statements.

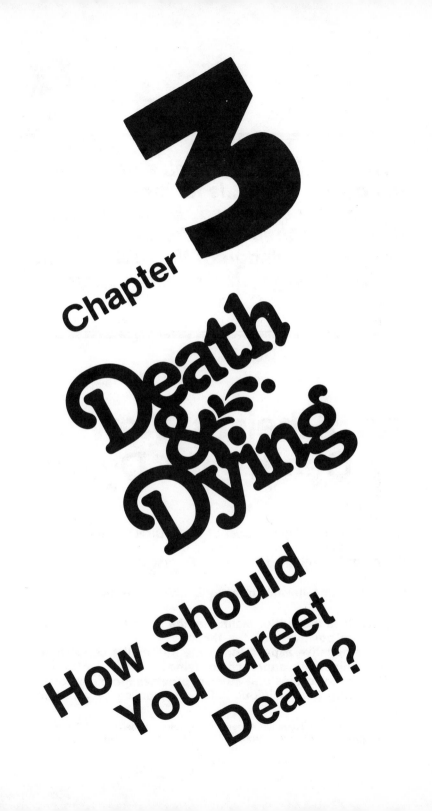

Chapter **3**

Death & Dying

How Should You Greet Death?

"The religionists' promise of something after death...is far more distressing to all concerned, both for the dying and their friends, than the certain knowledge of the atheists who realize a large size mammal simply died."

An Atheist's View of Death and Dying

Lloyd Thoren

Lloyd Thoren holds the post of State Director for American Atheists. A resident of Petersburg, Indiana, he is a director of the American Atheist Museum in Petersburg.

Consider the following questions while reading:

1. Why does the author claim that the atheist's view of death is more positive than the theist's?
2. What negative aspects does the author list concerning the religionist's approach to dying?
3. The author claims that atheism provides more support for the dying than religious belief. Do you agree with him?

Lloyd Thoren, "The Negative Aspects of Religion in the Area of Death and Dying", *American Atheist*, March, 1977. Reprinted with permission.

ATHEISM'S POSITIVE VIEWPOINT

This paper is written for the express purpose to show in the area—death and dying—the reasons Atheism is a positive viewpoint as contrasted with the theism's negative effects, on all of us still considered the living.

Atheism is seemingly hard, pragmatic, and based on facts as they exist in our present state of knowledge. In nature, like it or not, cripples simply do not live. No mouse or cat or bird knows the irrational idea that man blindly follows, that of self-sacrifice. In our culture, vast amounts of time and energy are wasted on the sacred altar; life has value, any life, however miserable. Some doctors recently have realized their work is to promote and perpetuate useful life, not a life of continuing misery...

Often the point is made to Atheists, "Just wait until you are sick or dying and you will beg for help." That's hogwash. It's only been in the last 100 years that man knew of pain-killing drugs and the electrical devices used to keep the dying alive one more day. For what? The simple truth is that the dying have not only no value, but they take much time and effort, all for nothing, so that the end result is that they have a negative value.

The religionists encourage self-sacrifice, feelings of abjection, as well as the wretched lie about a life after death. We are, for the most part, "in the dark ages", philosophically, but now with automobiles and electrical lights...

RELIGION'S NEGATIVISM

In the past, many stories grew and developed, and are perpetuated, **primarily to give comfort to those witnessing the death of a loved one**, but also to comfort the dying.

This paper will be an attempt to point out the negative aspects of certain religious ideologies: promising a heaven, threatening a hell, a reincarnation, a possible resurrection at some future date, or any of the other myths popularly believed by many. It affects those dying as well as the living friends of that person.

Most of us know that much of the way we thought of our universe many generations ago was in error, and as our knowledge increases, we correct our previously erroneous beliefs. This means that any thinking man understands the

hazards of believing something to be true, no matter how many join in complete agreement. The way one thinks is right may not be, and this nagging doubt will cause continuing serious anxiety because no proofs of life after death exist. All such beliefs — life after death — have been assertions, heresay from second, third, or fourth hand proclamations, often by unknown other people.

The early thinking that years ago the earth was believed to be flat was proved wrong when it was discovered to be a sphere, and the belief that the earth was the center of the universe was proved false. Recently even in this generation, we speak of the sun rising and setting when we know it's the turning of the earth that makes it appear that way.

From this we know that any of our present conceptions could be sometime proven wrong. Lucky for us in small things this doesn't count for much, but in a matter of life and death the ugly spectacle of fear looms large and no amount of reassurance seems capable of alleviating this fear.

It is truly cruel to make a promise of a happy life after death and then provide absolutely no positive proof of it. The recipient of such a promise is far worse off than if such an idea was never presented until proven.

The most agonizing part of dying is attempting to hope for something after death and at the same time maintaining the serious doubts that one could be wrong in this thinking, and there may be nothing after death. In Elisabeth Kubler-Ross's book, **On Death and Dying**, on pages 265–266, it says:

"Religious patients seemed to differ little from those without a religion. The difference may be hard to determine, since we have not clearly defined what we mean by a religious person. We can say here, however, that we found very few truly religious people with an intrinsic faith. Those few have been helped by their faith and are best comparable with those few patients who were true Atheists. The majority of patients were in between, with some form of religious belief, but not enough to relieve them of conflict and fear." **(Ross, 1969).**

This means we have a small group on the one extreme, the Atheists, and the serious theists on the other, but the large majority of both the living and dying are in the middle group. For the living in good health, there is little to worry about because there is time to perhaps resolve doubts.

For the terminally ill, the dying, their time is running out. This fear of what comes next suddenly grows into enormous proportions. The certain knowledge of the extreme groups, the theists or the Atheists, has not been resolved by the doubter.

It is clear, having learned of a situation, gives relief whether bad or good for the individual, compared with suffering a paranoid uncertainty which lingers and seems to magnify. (A tumor may or may not be malignant, and the worry while the biopsy is in the lab is considerable.)

RELIGION AND DEATH

Therefore, I conclude that the religionists' promise of something after death, which apparently a majority doubt, is far more distressing to all concerned, both for the dying and their friends, than the certain knowledge of the Atheists who realize a large size mammal simply died.

It is truly cruel to make a promise of a happy life after death and then provide absolutely no positive proof of it. The recipient of such a promise is far worse off than if such an idea was never presented until proven.

Another negative aspect of religion on the dying is the stern, serious, almost morbid ceremony laid on the dying, that which is called last rites. At the very time when everyone in the vicinity of the dying are already saddened, in comes a priest or preacher to pray or mumble words which are most often incomprehensible to those who are involved.

On pages 102-105 of **Doctrines and Discipline of The Evangelical Church**, published in 1935, is a typical Christian burial service. My grandfather, the Reverend Herman Henry Thoren, would have said a part or all of the following:

"As it has pleased the Lord, in whose power are life and death, to remove the soul of the departed from time to eternity, we commit the body to the cold earth. When we are called upon to depart this life, we may rest in Him Who is our hope, and that in the general resurrection at the last day, we may be found in Him, and receive from Him, the gift of eternal life. May He, Who has the power over life and death, enable you to obtain an abundant entrance into His heavenly kingdom." **(Doctrines, Discipline, 1935.)**

Whatever possible comfort this could provide, other than the soothing effect of a monotonous voice babbling a repetitive incantation, is more than offset by the mind-boggling theological concepts of an all-powerful Lord, removing a soul (absolutely impossible to conceptualize) to a heavenly kingdom which cannot be visualized or described, however great may one's powers of imagination be.

MISS PEACH by Mell Lazarus. Courtesy of Mell Lazarus and Field Newspaper Syndicate.

The complete sense of bewilderment would undoubtedly cause one to feel hopelessly lost in a fog, when in fact, existentially, the reality is, a loved one simply died. The absurdity of attempting to explain meeting a dead loved one at some future date, at some given age, in some nebulous place, is so very clearly evident, that a person who has chosen to stop thinking about anything, could, in an almost comatose state, agree that anything is possible.

At this point, while writing this paper, I am finding that I have fallen into the environmental traps. So completely have I been indoctrinated that I may have used words like departed, passed on, no longer with us, as well as many other similar phrases. Fortunately, I caught myself and used the more accurate word, dead.

The probable most serious negative aspect of religion, as it relates to death and dying, is that its practitioners or clergy enter the scene only at this and other crucial times in the life cycle. The Last Rites of the Catholic Church is a good example of this...

I can understand a small minority being so psychotic that heaven and/or hell seem to them to be reality. However, the average individual strives often desperately to maintain contact with reality. If a serious psychotic can face death with contentment, does that justify the agony of the majority, who can't conceptualize heaven, hell, or a soul? I think not. The torment of their minds when terminally ill, along with those loving them and watching, is not worth the insane pleasure of so few who buy the propaganda of eternal life...

To conclude, to die slowly with **doubted** happy delusions is a hell far worse than facing the fact, "All we know is living; death is unending nothingness. You have today to live graciously, beautifully, richly. This life is the only life you have."

"Only when we face death head-on, with all its 'dread and fascination,' does the power of the gospel message of Jesus really hit us with the full impact of its promise and hope."

A Christian's View of Death and Dying

William Toohey

William Toohey, CSC, is director of campus ministry at the University of Notre Dame and the author of several books.

Consider the following questions while reading:

1. What does the author mean when he says, "we come face to face with death all the time"?
2. Why does the author caution against viewing death as the final step toward full life?
3. The author claims that our own resurrection is more important than immortality. What does he mean? Do you agree?

William Toohey, "The Decision for Death...and Life", *America*, December 11, 1976. Reprinted with permission of America Press, Inc., 106 West 56th Street, New York, N.Y. 10019. © 1976 All rights reserved.

In a way, I suspect we'd all rather not talk about death. Man has been trying to deal with death through all the ages, making attempts to soften its blow, eliminate the harshness of its inevitability and the pain of its experience. For example, men have sought for some sort of immortality through their progeny or by monuments erected to their accomplishments and heroic deeds. Others have attempted to compromise death's obliterating force by "living life to the hilt."...

WE FACE DEATH ALL THE TIME

Whether we relish it or not, we must talk about death. Faith's call necessitates we put to death our longing for certainty and our fear of risk. Our pledge of fidelity is the beginning of death—a dying to whatever stands between ourselves and our faithfulness to our promise. There is a certainty of death that follows from the efforts of a Christian to go outside of himself (and safety, comfort, convenience) to meet the needs of others. We are convinced that, in order to struggle for a new world of justice and peace, one needs to die to old values, attitudes and life styles, to popularity, notoriety and ready acceptance.

Thus, we come face to face with death all the time. It is interesting that the dying demanded in order to live the rich, full life to which God calls us finds a parallel in the life–death–life experiences of natural growth, from infancy through adolescence to adulthood and old age. Birth itself is death to life within the womb; and it is followed by a constant series of further death-in-order-to-know-fuller-life experiences. To go off to school, for instance, is to die to the security the youngster has known at home. The adolescent suffers the many deaths of decision–making, rejection and loneliness; and the adult, though more experienced now, still struggles with the deaths that are so much a part of the normal human condition.

It seems to follow from this that we should expect to see physical death as the last step toward full life. If the fullness of life is our destiny and physical death is the final step, then that death becomes movement away from death. There is much appeal in this. God is the God of the living. He has, we believe, been continually giving us more life every day (if we accept it), and would not be such a monster as to reverse His offers of life at the grave.

As attractive as this may seem, however, there are a couple of subtle traps in it. First of all, emphasizing death as the last step to full life can lead to the devaluation of the present life. It would be possible to see a great chasm between this present existence and our future. We could fall victim, as have so many Christians, to proponents of "pie in the sky"—endure your oppressed half-life now and God will reward you later.

NOTHING TO FEAR

The just have nothing to fear at the hour of death. If God holds them in his hands, who can snatch them from him? It is true that the powers of darkness try to tempt and attack even the saints at the hour of death. But it is also true that God continues to offer help—and even increases his graces—to his faithful servants at such a dangerous hour. As the Psalmist says: "The Lord is a stronghold...in times of distress" (Ps 9:10).

St. Alphonsus Liquori, *Preparation for Death.*

A concentration on life after death has led many people to depreciate this life. Frequently, it results in the employment of resurrection promises to shield one from the here-and-now struggle for a decent life. And oftentimes, too, there is an effort to obscure and hide from a person the full reality of death and its actual enormity. It is not at all healthy to try to play such games with death. Only when we face death head-on, with all its "dread and fascination," does the power of the gospel message of Jesus really hit us with the full impact of its promise and hope.

ETERNAL LIFE NOW

We are meant to experience God's eternal life now. It is none other than His resurrected life that Jesus shares with us: "I am the resurrection and the life; he who believes in me, though he be dead, shall live; and whoever lives and believes in me shall never die at all." One of the chief problems for man is the temptation to succumb to a conspiracy against the present tense, that is, the tendency to push off to some future time what is intended as a present reality. In some real sense, then, resurrection is an experience God has planned for us now, because intimate life with Him is meant to begin now. That is why St. John can say: "Even in this world we have become as He is." The saints always considered heaven a present reality; they correctly understood it as "belonging to God," something that occurs when we wholeheartedly consent to the Father who loves unconditionally...

There is another trap, however. Besides overlooking the splendor and significance of this present time through an overemphasis on future life, one can make the opposite mistake. To concentrate on the fact that we are destined to enjoy Jesus' risen life now, could make us believe that present life is "continued" after death. It is the trap of thinking that immortality is the principal issue.

"For eye has not seen nor has ear heard, nor has it entered into the heart of man what God has prepared for those who love Him."

Every springtime, as we observe the marvelous rebirth of nature, we may increasingly doubt that death has the final say. This "evidence" of immortality is seemingly bolstered by the investigations of the scientific community. Led by noted psychiatrist Elisabeth Kubler-Ross, explorations of the experiences of people resuscitated after being declared clinically dead are said to confirm belief in immortality.

The "evidence" for life after death introduced by Dr. Kubler-Ross and others is, of course, scientifically unverifiable. But suppose we could verify that there was life after death. Is this really the crucial question? I think not.

Dr. Kubler-Ross and her colleagues suggest that the reality of eternal life is fortified by stories of patients who have "died" and reported back. But immortality is not the Christian destiny. The gospel does not proclaim mere endless existence, even when that existence would mean a continuation, as we noted above, of a life already enriched by Jesus' risen life. There is still something more in store for us—our own resurrection!

IMMORTALITY AND RESURRECTION

We must not confuse immortality with resurrection. If immortality (life merely continued after death) is what we set our sights on, we may feel no need for the Easter experience that is meant to be ours. Resurrection for Jesus was far more than "picking up where He left off." He was "a new creation"; He was "in glory." Right now we are meant to be alive with God's own life, filled with His spirit and enriched with His presence, and that's marvelous! But all of that is as nothing compared with what awaits us: "For eye has not seen nor has ear heard, nor has it entered into the heart of man what God has prepared for those who love Him."...

And we can dare to believe that, because of the risen life we experience, death and hatred and despair will not have the last word. No, the last word is not "exit" but "entrance," not "dearly departed" but "newly arrived," not "Sorry about that" but "Welcome home!"

"Confronted by the final mystery, man may be afraid, but by making a joke he can prove that he has not collapsed in panic."

Facing Death With Humor

Jay Weiss

Jay Weiss is an orthodontist and writer from Caldwell, New Jersey.

Consider the following questions while reading:
1. **Why does the author think humor can help the dying person face death? Do you agree?**
2. **Do you think gallows humor is blasphemous or an example of human dignity?**

Jay Weiss, "Last Words." This article first appeared in *The Humanist*, November/December 1976 and is reprinted by permission.

"Do you think one who has known how to live honorably for eighty years does not know how to die for a quarter of an hour?"

—Anne de Montmorency

Instead of being the central actor in a significant process, today's terminally ill patient is left to die in isolation, surrounded not by grieving relatives but by the paraphernalia of an unfeeling science. This medical machinery not only robs modern man of his own death, as Aries puts it, but it may also have choked off another time–honored phenomenon: the dying man's last words.

Relatively unencumbered by medical devices, failing wits of earlier days were sometimes able to face death with detachment and good humor, or, at least, so it seemed. The best of them managed to sum up a lifetime in one or two terminal phrases.

WILSON MIZNER

Wilson Mizner, the celebrated American bon vivant, con man, promoter, and occasional writer, was a good example. He began training for the final bout at a tender age. From the start, Mizner viewed death with studied irreverence. In his splendid biography, *The Legendary Mizners*, Alva Johnston writes that Wilson's "comic style was largely ridicule of all sentiment and feeling... Death was the finest of all comedy subjects, because it provided the largest amount of emotion to be deflated."

Long before his hour actually came, Wilson tuned up with tentative last words. When, after much fussing and fulminating against predatory "croakers and sawbones," he finally agreed to have an inflamed appendix removed, he first issued careful instructions for a possible funeral. "Have my coffin," he ordered, "fit well around the shoulders."

Much later, Mizner was told by his brother, Addison, that another brother had been killed in an automobile accident. Wilson complained, "Why didn't you tell me before I put on a red tie?"

Soon after, Addison himself grew gravely ill. Wilson promptly wired him, "Stop dying. Am trying to write a comedy." This advice was distinctly less sentimental than Mizner's famous reaction to the death of Stanley Ketchel, a scrappy young boxer he had managed. Ketchel had been shot dead by

72

a jealous husband. "Tell 'em to start counting ten over him, and he'll get up," said Mizner.

When his own turn came, Wilson rose to the occasion, as well as could be expected under the circumstances. Recovering consciousness after a heart attack, he replied expansively to the inquiry, "Do you want a priest?"

"I want a priest," he said, "a rabbi, and a Protestant clergyman. I want to hedge my bets." His heart attack, the inauguration of F.D.R., the bank holiday, and an earthquake in California had occurred almost simultaneously. Mizner's considerable experience in the theater led him to protest this wild profusion of climaxes. "Bad melodrama," he said.

Told that death was close, he gathered enough strength to write a friend. "They're going to bury me at 9 A.M. Don't be a sucker and get up."

An oxygen tent was set up for him. "Looks like the main event," he commented. Mizner sank into a coma and rallied. He waved away a priest, "Why should I talk to you when I've just been talking to your boss?" The priest protested that this was a poor time to make jokes. Death might be only minutes away. "What," complained Mizner, "no two weeks notice?"

RALEIGH, FREUD, THOREAU, SHAW

Sir Walter Raleigh met death with at least as much aplomb. In his time, Raleigh had been an adventurer, explorer, wit, writer, and notorious religious skeptic. Now he was about to be beheaded. He asked the executioner if he might examine the ax. He ran his thumb along the edge. Smiling, he said to the astounded sheriff, "This is a sharp medicine, but it is a sure cure for all diseases."

Asked if he would not prefer to face the east, where the Lord had risen, Raleigh replied, "So the heart is right, it is no matter which way the head lieth." Still, to satisfy his friends, he faced east. But he refused a blindfold. "Think you I fear the shadow of the ax when I fear not the ax itself?"

Overwhelmed by this gallantry, the executioner hesitated. Raleigh encouraged him. "What dost thou fear?" he asked. "Strike, man, strike."

Several centuries later, in September, 1939, another religious skeptic, Sigmund Freud, was asked by his doctor if he thought the great war that had just broken out would be the last one.

"*My* last war," was Freud's brief reply. Max Schur reports that Freud's later request for a quick release from intractable pain was made "without a trace of emotionality or self-pity and with full consciousness of reality."

Henry David Thoreau was a transcendentalist, not a skeptic. Nevertheless, this amiable position alarmed one of his aunts, a strict Calvinist. She asked the dying Thoreau if he had made his peace with God. Thoreau replied that he had never quarreled with Him...

When George Bernard Shaw was near death, the BBC was moved to make a special offer. They called his house. "We know that Mr. Shaw listens to the Third Programme and enjoys the music. We should like to play for him something he would especially like to hear—a symphony by Beethoven or a concert by Mozart, perhaps." The suggestion was conveyed to GBS. "Tell him to play 'The Old Cow Died,'" Shaw said.

While it terrifies many, imminent death would not appear to hold any terrors for others. In 1906, just before he lapsed into a coma, the German-American founder of civil service, Carl Shurz, remarked, *"Es ist so einfach zu sterben!"* This was virtually the same sentiment expressed on his deathbed more than a century earlier by the great English doctor William Hunter: "If I could hold a pen I would write how easy and pleasant a thing it is to die," he said...

Eugene Labiche, the nineteenth-century French playwright, was presented with the following request by one of his relatives, a pious widower: "You who are going to see my wife again in Paradise, tell her please, that I love her still and that I think of her constantly."

Labiche replied, "Listen, really, you can run your little errands yourself."

Jean Louis Forain, a French satirical artist, was dying and his doctor was examining him regularly. "Frankly, Mr. Forain, I find you in much better shape than yesterday. Your temperature is normal, your pulse is regular, and your blood pressure is fine." "Yes, to sum up," concluded Forain, "I shall die cured."

Claude Favre de Vaugelas, the illustrious grammarian, at the very moment of his death, went right on parsing. "I go," he said, "or I am going." In a murmur he explained, "One or the other is said" —then, releasing a final sigh, he added, "or are said."

Guitry professed particular admiration for Sebastien Chamfort, who, like Raleigh, Freud, and Mizner, was a religious skeptic. Chamfort wished at all costs to avoid receiving the last rites. As he expired, he explained his scheme to avoid them. "I am going to pretend," he whispered in the ear of one of his friends, "that I am not dying."

LAST WORDS

Despite their charm, such memorable last words were probably just as infrequent in France as they were everywhere else. Most people slip into a coma or a gravely weakened condition long before they actually pass on. Accordingly, the great majority of last words are relatively incoherent or commonplace. And who among us would choose to preserve his faculties to the last so as to deliver one final, unforgettable witticism if it meant paying the price exacted of a Nathan Hale or a Walter Raleigh?

But the possibility that some significant statement or thought might be expressed added to the ceremonial value of the traditional deathbed scene and offered a kind of solace to the bereaved. Modern science now takes away even that slim chance...

Are such remarks merely frivolous, even blasphemous, as Wilson Mizner's priest suggested? Perhaps. But there is another way to look at gallows humor. Confronted by the final mystery, man may be afraid, but by making a joke he can prove that he has not collapsed in panic. What better way is there to express the essential dignity of the human spirit than by keeping our wits about us to the very end, even in the face of the great unknown from which we came and into which we must all disappear?

"We should not fear death, for then we cease to live fully now. Our desire not to die — to live forever or live again — must be put away lest we not, live at all."

A Religious Naturalist Looks at Death

Doris Webster Havice

Doris Webster Havice is professor emeritus of religious studies at the University of Colorado.

Consider the following questions while reading:
1. **Why does the author consider herself a "religious naturalist"?**
2. **The author claims people can respond to death in three ways. What are they?**
3. **What criticism does the author have for traditional religious and philosophical views of death?**
4. **What does the author think about the human wish to live after death?**

Doris Webster Havice, "A Religious Naturalist Looks at Death". Copyright 1975 Christian Century Foundation. Reprinted by permission from the November, 1975 issue of *The Christian Century*.

There have usually been two problems in understanding death: on the one hand, the belief that life is rendered meaningless if it is cut off in death and, on the other hand, the belief that human beings, unlike other animals, are too valuable to suffer the fate that awaits all other living forms.

Underlying both these beliefs is the assumption of a radical disjunction between humanity and the rest of nature with regard to value; being and destiny. I would challenge the assumption that human beings are in any way outside of, radically different from, or even more valuable than the total nexus of which we are a part. I call myself a naturalist because I cannot conceive of any useful theory that makes humankind unnatural. I call myself a religious naturalist because I am sure that the religious values of transcendence and ultimacy can best be preserved on the basis of this unitary assumption.

There are three responses which mortals can make in regard to death: to deny it, to accept it as an unpleasant but inevitable fact, or to affirm it not only as inevitable but also as a valid and joyous part of the natural process of which birth, living and death are equally important. I favor the third position. However, a brief review of the more orthodox positions, pointing out why from my viewpoint they fall short of validity, is in order.

DENYING DEATH

One way of denying death stems from Plato. In *The Republic* he writes: "The wise man will not count this life of man a matter of much concern, so for such a man death will have no terrors." In this view, life becomes a poor adumbration of true life, which comes after death. This attitude found its way into Christianity via neo–Platonism and persists among many orthodox Christians today. The Buddhist position is that all life is suffering which one can overcome only by realizing that the suffering results from attachment to the ego; thus, ridding oneself of the illusion of self makes death an illusion.

The orthodox Christian and the orthodox Buddhist both regard this life as a preparation for another kind of life, although the Christian seeks to purify the self while the Buddhist carries the purification so far as to be rid of self altogether. In neither case is life, here and now, taken seriously enough. Both views seem to lead to a kind of covert escapism from what I would call the real business of living...

MASTER OF DEATH

In all of this the point was quite simple: the dying person was not to be deprived of his death, rather he was to preside over it! Man was master of his life, he should also be master of his death.

Donald J. Moore, "The Final and Grandest Act," *America*, September, 1975.

A more recent denial of death that has attracted some attention is the position taken by Alan Harrington in *The Immortalist* (Avon, 1970), which, appropriately enough, first appeared in *Playboy*. Harrington maintains that life could be made over to eliminate death altogether through human engineering (genetic and otherwise). Going even further, he says that "the primary source of our fears, and all evil and meanness afflicting the human spirit...was death all the time, and nothing else." This new version of the Fountain of Youth myth seems about as attractive as the prospect of sitting on a cloud playing a harp and consuming milk and honey throughout eternity.

One could raise an almost inexhaustible number of questions; at least a few of them should be noted. At what point in the life cycle (or death cycle) would one wish to be stabilized? Considering the problem of overpopulation, it would seem necessary—if human engineering did not alter the reproductive cycle—to fix human life before puberty or after menopause. Can one imagine a valuable, or even interesting, existence if growth for everyone were halted at either of these two developmental levels? Who could really wish for the monotony that would be a necessary consequence of our being rendered immortal in this curiously naive sense?...

EXISTENTIALISM AND DEATH

At least since Epicurus some have viewed death as obviously the end, and the conviction that it is not is merely immature wishful thinking. To Freud, belief in immortality was part of what he called a socialized neurosis from which humanity would eventually recover. The existentialists make an ethical obligation of the notion that death is all and that "living in the face of death means living in such fashion that life can be broken off at any moment and not be rendered meaningless by such an accident."...

There is something very attractive about the existentialist position. To face life naked of any solace seems brave and upstanding. Perhaps, better than almost anyone else, the existentialist expresses the individual's responsibility to live well now. However, anyone who is aware of natural process will find that position unrealistic. Atheistic existentialism holds that there is no meaning in the universe apart from our obligation to create meaning in our own lives—and somehow that seems very pretentious...

ACCEPT DEATH TO FULLY LIVE

Death and life are inexorably bound up with each other. If we deny one, we deny the other and will inevitably live poorly (in the sense of less than fully)...

We know that, biologically, death begins in embryo. There is a constant sloughing off and generation of body tissues, a process that goes on throughout what we call life and continues after we die. Spiritually a similar process seems to be natural. We die to the old and are born to the new throughout life. Some of these deaths and births are more cataclysmic than others, but whether dramatic or gradual, the process of spiritual living is essentially the same as that of bodily living.

It is essential that each of us be aware that we make —or rather, contribute to—what is eternal. We should not fear death, for then we cease to live fully now. Our desire not to die—to live forever or live again—must be put away lest we not live at all.

Moreover, as we know, that which went together to make us what we are biologically was a product of a long existence before we were born, and whatever we are biologically will nourish and develop long after we die. But our influence on our world also goes on producing changes long after we are forgotten. As we live, we nourish or poison the lives around us, although to most of us it is not clear how or to what extent or in what ways. But each of us knows in his or her heart that this is so. In our most conscious moments we feel our responsibility to be aware of the meaning we have for others.

But many are unsatisfied with this description of meaning and value. Many want to persist as self-conscious selves.

Why? The problem here seems to be a profoundly ethical one. Jesus said that one must lose his life to find it. The Buddha said that one must outgrow attachment to the self. Many Christians seem to turn Jesus' admonition around and seek so hard to find themselves that they never lose themselves. And, as many Buddhist writers warn, to strive for detachment is to fail to reach it.

There is a Taoist story that illustrates the ethical problem. Two men are walking together when they notice that a man ahead of them has dropped his umbrella. They pick it up and hand it to him. But, says the teacher, this act is not a good one if the men who pick up the umbrella are interested in gratitude from the umbrella-dropper, or if they feel satisfaction for the act. In other words, the only really good act is one in which the self has been forgotten. This tale, it seems to me, applies equally well to the desire for personal immortality. One who feels the need to be recognized, to be a self in the hereafter to watch what happens, is not really living fully. Just as it seemed to the Hindu that for the good life to eventuate, ambition and competition must be relinquished and inner knowledge sought, so it seems that the only person who has really learned enough to live well is the one who has in some sense surmounted self...

It is essential that each of us be aware that we make—or rather, contribute to—what is eternal. We should not fear death, for then we cease to live fully now. Our desire not to die—to live forever or live again—must be put away lest we not live at all. Our need to be there in the future, to be "rewarded," vitiates our acts and turns them into ego trips instead of experiences of loving and living. We must return the umbrella without wanting to be noticed or we have done nothing for our neighbor, or our God.

SIX MONTHS TO LIVE

Pretend that you have been told by your doctor that you have an incurable disease and that you have no more than six months to live.

Instructions

STEP 1

Make a list of ten things you would want to do during your remaining six months. Next, rank your list in order of personal importance. Assign the number one (1) to the item considered most important, the number two (2) to the second most important item, and so on, until all the items have been ranked.

These are the ten things that I would like to do if I had only six months to live.

1. _____
2. _____
3. _____
4. _____
5. _____
6. _____
7. _____
8. _____
9. _____
10. _____

I would rank them in this order of importance.

1. _____ , 2. _____ , 3. _____ , 4. _____ , 5. _____ , 6. _____ , 7. _____ ,
8. _____ , 9. _____ , 10. _____ .

STEP 2

After you have finished your list, compare it with those compiled by other members of your class. Be sure to note the differences and similarities.

STEP 3

Form into groups of four to six students. Using your lists as a guide, discuss the following questions among yourselves:

1. What sort of things were mentioned most often? Least often?
2. What sort of things were ranked most important? Least important?
3. Would your list be different if the time left was not six months but six days or six years? Why?

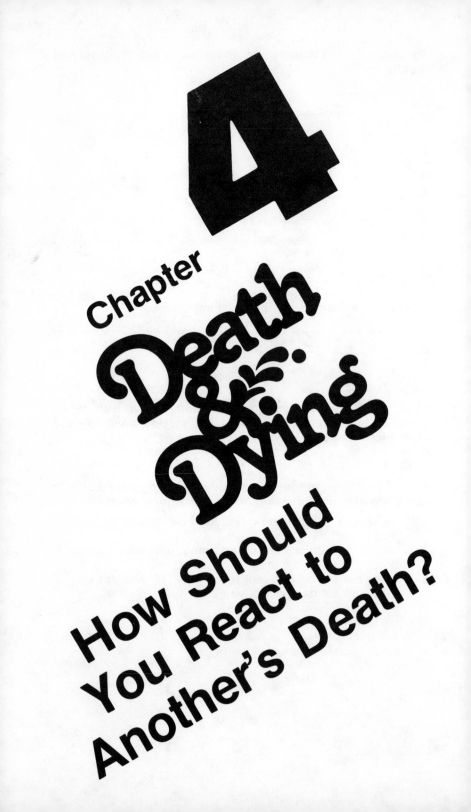

Chapter

4

Death & Dying

How Should You React to Another's Death?

"Grief is the other side of love. If you are capable of love you are capable of grief... Grief is normal for normal people."

Grief is Normal

Edgar N. Jackson

Edgar N. Jackson, a theologian and psychologist, is the author of *Understanding Grief*, *When Someone Dies* and *The Christian Funeral*.

Consider the following questions while reading:
1. **What is grief and why do we grieve for a loved one?**
2. **Why is it important to mourn properly?**
3. **Why does the author think grief and love are related?**
4. **How can grief become abnormal?**

Edgar N. Jackson, "Grief." From Earl A. Grollman, *Concerning Death: A Practical Guide for the Living.* Reprinted by permission of Beacon Press. Copyright © 1974 by Earl A. Grollman.

WHAT IS GRIEF?

Grief is the intense emotion that floods life when a person's inner security system is shattered by an acute loss, usually associated with the death of someone important in his/her life.

In more personal terms, grief is a young widow who must find a way to bring up her three children, alone. Grief is the angry reaction of a man so filled with shocked uncertainty and confusion that he strikes out at the nearest person. Grief is the little old lady who goes to the funeral of a stranger and does some unfinished business of her own feeling by crying her eyes out there; she is weeping for herself, for the event she is sure will come, and for which she has so little help in preparing herself.

Grief is a mother walking daily to a nearby cemetery to stand quietly alone for a few moments before she goes on about the tasks of the day; she knows that part of her is in the cemetery, just as part of her is in her daily work. Grief is the deep sympathy one person has for another when he wants to do all he can to help resolve a tragic experience. Grief is the silent, knifelike terror and sadness that comes a hundred times a day, when you start to speak to someone who is no longer there.

Grief is the emptiness that comes when you eat alone after eating with another for years. Grief is the desperate longing for another whose loss you cannot learn to endure. Grief is teaching yourself how to go to bed without saying good night to the one who has died. Grief is the helpless wishing that things were different when you know they are not and never will be again. Grief is a whole cluster of adjustments, apprehensions, and uncertainties that strike life in its forward progress and make it difficult to reorganize and redirect the energies of life.

Grief is always more than sorrow. Bereavement is the event in personal history that triggers the emotion of grief. Mourning is the process by which the powerful emotion is slowly and painfully brought under control. But when doctors speak of grief they are focusing on the raw feelings that are at the center of a whole process that engages the person in adjusting to changed circumstances. They are speaking of the deep fears of the mourner, of his prospects of loneliness, and of the obstacles he must face as he finds a new way of living.

WHY DO WE GRIEVE FOR A LOVED ONE WHO DIED?

Usually we do not grieve for the person who has died but rather for ourselves and our own sense of loss. The person who has died is no longer able to use his nervous system to feel physical pain. The person who is still alive and capable of feeling has the emotional response. It is usually a conflicted feeling because he suffers the loss and at the same time has the basic human response of being glad that he is still alive and able to experience sensations even though they may be painful. So grief is usually characterized by ambivalence—of two conflicting types of sensation going on at the same time. As St. Augustine pointed out, grief is a strange mixture of joy and sorrow — joy to be yet alive and sorrow to have life diminished by the loss of one we love.

SEARCH FOR MEANING

We must be allowed to grieve over the tragic as well as the beautiful. In grieving we search for meaning in the mystery of life.

Father Dennis J. Geaney, "Give in to Grief," *U. S. Catholic,* February, 1978.

We grieve because we experience deprivation. Our life has been diminished. We have lost something we cherished and we do not want to admit the loss. Life is made up of deprivation experiences, for every time we make a choice we give up one alternative in order to accept the other. But death is so final and so overwhelming a deprivation that our past experience does not seem to adequately prepare us for its personal devastation. We feel that part of our own being is lost with our deprivation. Because a part of our inner being was invested in another, we have this feeling of being personally reduced.

That is why it is so important to do the work of mourning wisely and well, for it is through this process that we retrieve that part of ourself so that we can continue life as a whole person rather than as one who has been permanently diminished because of his/her loss. Mourning is the process that guarantees that we happen to our grief rather than having our grief happen to us. Mourning is the process of self-mastery that makes sure we remain whole, even though deprived, rather than being destroyed by what has happened to us. Our grief is rooted in emotions that reach out in all directions beyond our physical being. Only as we literally pull up by the roots the feelings that no longer have a soil to sustain them are we able to let them take root again elsewhere and be nurtured with life–giving experience...

IS GRIEF NORMAL?

Grief is the other side of the coin of love. If you are capable of love you are capable of grief. Only the person who is incapable of loving another is entirely free of the possibility of grief. We would not want to think of life without love. But when you love you become vulnerable, because the one you love may suffer and die and part of you suffers and dies along with him. When anyone dies we all die a little, for we are all diminished and reminded of our own mortal status. But this is not a hopeless state; the death we experience in our grief can be overcome at least in part by healthful mourning whereby our inner being is restored to normal. So grief is normal for normal people.

IS THERE A DISTINCTION BETWEEN NORMAL AND ABNORMAL GRIEF?

Yes, for with normal grief you are able to work your way back to productive and near normal living, while with abnormal grief you develop a chronic state of psychological or physical symptoms that persist for an unreasonable period of time.

Soon after a death, it is difficult to separate the normal from the abnormal. Under the stress of powerful emotions, people say and do things that are quite out of character. We must ask ourselves, then, whether an act that may seem abnormal is part of a whole pattern of unusual actions and reactions or merely an isolated occurrence. And we want to see whether this new way of acting and reacting is becoming more firmly fixed or less so.

The abnormal usually shows up in extremes. Sometimes what we observe is a seeming inability to react emotionally at all. The person who is cold, efficient, impersonal, and dry–eyed under powerful emotional stress may be under-reacting. The person who goes all to pieces may be over-reacting. We cannot on the face of it say that the seemingly calm person is handling his situation well; neither can we say, in the face of an explosion of grief, that sorrow is shattering to the other.

GRIEF AND MOURNING

Grief and mourning have to do with being abandoned and with loss. They are the natural consequences of the loss of boundaries. All grief and mourning is about severed connectedness, which gets translated in how we do or don't make endings. Grief is the feeling of loss at the interrupted or broken connection, and mourning is the process of incorporating that loss into our lives. Grief usually begins with the unexpected, and is the emotional expression of this newly-created space or ended connection. Mourning is the process of working through that grief.

Stanley Keleman, *Living Your Dying.*

If the mourner has emotional weak spots in his nature, they may show in aggravated form under the pressure of grief. Danger signals one must watch for are unreasonable withdrawal from normal functions, excessive anger at others, or intense suspicion of others. Anger and/or suspicion may be directed against the physician, the minister, the funeral director, or even toward members of the immediate family. Moods of inappropriate elation or deep depression may also indicate that things are not right.

One of the best ways to gauge abnormal emotional reactions is to observe a person's behavior a month or so after the death. Most people will be quite back to normal by that time. If physical and emotional symptoms persist, and if the person is unable to function effectively after a few weeks, it is a fairly specific indication that he should have some special help in meeting his problems of adjustment.

The exception here might be widows or widowers, where the basic problems of adjustment involve so much of life, its status, and its role relationships, that a longer period of readjustment may well be within the norm.

GRIEF CENTER

The above design is the logo for a grief center located in Burnsville, Minnesota. This center, like others across the United States, offers counseling and guidance to people during periods of bereavement. Richard J. Obershaw, a psychotherapist who is director of the Burnsville Center, has authored a booklet entitled *Death Dying Grief and Funerals*. A copy of the booklet may be obtained by sending $2.00 to:

Grief Center
318 Riverwoods Lane
Burnsville, MN 55337

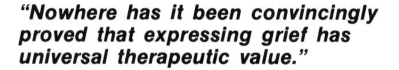

"Nowhere has it been convincingly proved that expressing grief has universal therapeutic value."

Is Expressing Grief Always Necessary?

Norman Klein

Norman Klein is associate professor of anthropology at California State University in Los Angeles. He is the editor of *Culture, Curers and Contagion.*

Consider the following questions while reading:
1. **Why does the author claim expressions of grief may not be helpful?**
2. **What does the author mean when he claims that we may be in danger of "replacing old myths and stereotypes with new myths and stereotypes"?**
3. **Do you think a person who does not openly express grief can still be normal?**

In our own society, faddish therapies stress the idea that openly expressing sorrow, anger, or pain is a good thing, and the only means for "dealing with one's feelings honestly." "Holding things in" comes to be seen as deviant.

Yet nowhere has it been convincingly proved that expressing grief has universal therapeutic value. Perhaps more important, this insistence on the requirement to feel and tell represents an ethnocentric standard that can do injustice to persons and groups who cope differently.

GRIEF AND DENIAL

Americans are said to fear and deny death, and if the denial becomes complete, it requires "defenses which can only be destructive," in the words of Elisabeth Kubler–Ross. She is perhaps best known for her scheme of the five stages of a "complete" death: (1) denial, (2) anger, (3) bargaining, (4) depression, and (5) acceptance. Each stage has a transitional value—taken alone, for instance, denial is seen as bad, though as a temporary buffer it is good—and, given enough time, a patient can reach a point of accepting death.

Kubler-Ross's work is undoubtedly useful; it may even help family, friends, and professionals to assist the dying patient who has the emotional needs she describes.

Yet it is surely conceivable that some Americans can work through grief internally or privately, without psychological cost; it is even more conceivable that whole cultural subgroups may have different ways of conceiving and responding to such experience. Harvard psychiatrist Ned H. Cassem has questioned the generally negative view of denial espoused by Kubler–Ross. "Denial can be a constructive force, enabling people to put out of mind morbid, frightening, and depressing aspects of life."

STANDARDS MAY BE ARBITRARY

A cross–cultural perspective reveals how arbitrary any one such standard may be. In 1976, psychologists Paul Rosenblatt, Patricia Walsh, and Douglas Jackson used the Human Relations Area Files, a massive compendium of anthropological data, to examine mourning in a large number of societies. They found in their review of 73 societies that what varies is the form and intensity of its expression. In 72 societies, people weep at death; the Balinese say they laugh to avoid crying. Are the Balinese unhealthy?

CONTINUING PAIN

Toxic grief is a mourning process that directs the individual to the past, to what has been or is about to be lost. It provokes continuing pain having to do with separation. The individual becomes grief-stricken, immersed in the suffering of bereavement. The griever often experiences repeated emotional and mental fantasies associated with the deceased. Life fluctuates between the real and the imagined. Sometimes there are suicidal impulses.

Gerald A. Larue, "Grief," *The Humanist,* July/August, 1978.

The researchers also correlated gender differences in crying for 60 societies: in 32 of them, both sexes cried equally; in the 28 in which there was a difference, it was always the women who cried more. Are they healthier?

In 18 of 32 societies, self-injury (such as cutting off a finger at a joint) is regularly attempted by both grieving men and women; women self-mutilate more in 12. But if emotional letting go is a good thing, should men and women, equally, mutilate themselves even more frequently?

Closer to home, psychologist Richard Kalish and anthropologist David Reynolds compared the attitudes on death and mourning of black Americans, Japanese-Americans, Mexican-Americans, and white Americans in Los Angeles. Asked if they would "try very hard to control the way you showed your emotions in public," the groups offered a wide range of responses. Japanese and black respondents said they would (82 percent, 79 percent) more often than white Americans and Mexican-Americans, for example (74 percent, 64 percent).

Japanese-Americans, who are most frequently reticent about public grief, would seem to bear out the stereotypic notion of Orientals as stoic. Public-health nurse Thelma Dobbins Payne reports that the reluctance of many Japanese-American women to cry out during childbirth leads some non-Japanese physicians to "wonder if Japanese women feel the pain." Japanese-American physicians, however, described a common alternative style in labor: "wincing," "grimacing," "frowning."

How much and what type of emoting is necessary to avoid the label "stoic"? The real issue rests with the way the various cultures define the appropriate expression of emotion. At the same time, it is very important to note that in no group Kalish and Reynolds studied was there a 100 percent agreement by all informants—sex, age, religion, and education all affected the responses.

"Death with dignity" and "a beautiful death" verge on becoming the new jargon of concern. But for whom are these expressions really meaningful? Do they describe the dying person's experience, or the observer's? Attitudes toward death are clearly influenced by culture—and by subculture, and by individual personality. It follows, then, that we must take care not to formalize or prescribe the way in which people express emotion. As Kalish and Reynolds remark in their discussion, "This era is in danger of replacing old myths and stereotypes with new myths and stereotypes, slightly more accurate and less destructive perhaps, but nonetheless not always appropriate."

"Ordinary grief constitutes a syndrome that runs a predictable course through three definable stages. The manifestations of grief during each stage serve an important function for the bereaved and are necessary way stations along his return to a normal life."

The Three Stages of Grief

Robert B. White and Leroy T. Gathman

Dr. Robert B. White is professor of psychiatry in the Department of Psychiatry and Behavioral Sciences and director of Postgraduate Education in Psychiatry at the University of Texas Medical Branch in Galveston, Texas. Dr. White originally wrote this viewpoint in a longer article that appeared in *American Family Physician* and was intended to assist doctors who are treating bereaved persons. He is senior author of the following viewpoint.

Consider the following questions while reading:
1. **What does the author claim are the three stages of grief?**
2. **What treatment, recommended management, does he suggest in the accompanying chart?**
3. **How does Dr. White define grief?**

Robert B. White and Leroy T. Gatman, "The Syndrome of Ordinary Grief", *American Family Physician*. Reprinted with permission from the August, 1973 issue of *American Family Physician*, published by the American Academy of Family Physicians.

Ordinary grief constitutes a syndrome that runs a pre-dictable course through three definable stages *(see chart on page 97)*. The manifestations of grief during each stage serve an important function for the bereaved and are necessary way stations along his return to a normal life...

STAGE 1: SHOCK, NUMBNESS, DISBELIEF

Usually lasting for a period of minutes to a day or so, this stage is exemplified by the almost universal tendency to ex-claim, "Oh, no—I can't believe it," upon learning of the unexpected death of a beloved friend or relative. This stage of numb disbelief is caused by the human inability to accept easily or quickly the reality and finality of the separation imposed by death. This numbness protects the bereaved for a time and allows him to attend to various immediate matters related to the death...

STAGE 2: PAINFUL LONGING AND PREOCCUPATION WITH MEMORIES AND MENTAL IMAGES

This stage begins minutes, hours or days after the death and reaches its peak between the second and fourth weeks; it subsides gradually after that. The manifestations of this stage are intense for about three months, progressively de-clining over the next six to 12 months.

The most prominent aspect of this stage is the recurrent, wave-like experience of tearful longing for the deceased, associated with thoughts, memories or mental images of him. These waves are often triggered by any reminder of the dead person—a friend's comment, a place associated with the de-ceased or the time of day at which he returned home from work. Christmas, Thanksgiving and birthdays frequently pro-voke such episodes. These wave-like episodes tend to be expecially intense and painful at night, when the distractions of the day are removed.

In addition to preoccupation with memories and visual images of the deceased, about half of mourning spouses and parents have illusions of seeing or feeling the presence of the dead person...

The meaning of preoccupation with mental images of the deceased and of experiences in which the dead seem present is explained by current views on the function of grief. Grief is

Stages of Ordinary Grief

Timetable	Manifestations	Recommended Management
STAGE 1: Begins immediately after death, lasts one to three days	Shock Disbelief, denial Numbness Weeping Wailing Agitation	Home visit Arrange office visit Nighttime sedation Avoid daytime use of sedatives or tranquilizers
STAGE 2: Peaks between two to four weeks after death; begins to subside after three months, lasts up to one year	Painful longing Preoccupation Memories Mental images of the deceased Sense of the deceased being present Sadness Tearfulness Insomnia Anorexia Loss of interest Irritability Restlessness	Periodic office visits Encourage expression of feelings Explanation of grief process Reassurance that what bereaved feels is part of the normal grief process Nighttime sedation Avoid daytime use of sedatives or tranquilizers

(In rare cases of severe depression, consider [1] antidepressants, [2] hospitalization, [3] psychiatric consultation and [4] electroshock therapy)

STAGE 3: Should occur within a year after death	Resolution Decreasing episodes of sadness Ability to recall the past with pleasure Resumption of ordinary activities	When indicated, discussion of anniversary reaction

viewed as a process of gradual adaptation to the sudden and final separation from a loved one. This ultimate, total separation is too overwhelming to comprehend or accept all at once.

By holding on to images, memories and experiences of the seeming presence of the deceased, the mourner gradually says goodbye. He takes his sad parting, bit by bit, in a process like leaving a loved one for a long journey...

DENIAL, ANGER, RECONSTRUCTION

Many people have written about the three stages of grief. The first is denial, the second, anger, and the third is reconstruction. In the denial stage, the grieving person denies intellectually that the person is dead. Then the bereaved goes through a stage of becoming very angry. Finally, there is the reorganization stage, which normally starts three or four months after the loss.

Ronald Lee, from an interview with David Sutor, *U. S. Catholic*, September, 1978.

We can only stand the pain of parting by means of these gradual good-byes to our memories of the dead. If the pain of these waves of images and memories is avoided, the goodbye is never completed and the bereaved is impaired in his capacity to return his attention to the world of the living...

STAGE 3: RESOLUTION AND RESUMPTION OF ORDINARY LIFE ACTIVITIES

During the second six months of his grief, the bereaved progressively regains interest in the ordinary activities of his life and in social and business relations. He continues to experience periodic episodes of sadness and painful longings and memories, but they gradually fade as he becomes able to remember the past and talk of the deceased with equanimity and, eventually, with pleasure and interest. A significant number of grief-stricken spouses and parents, however, continue to feel great emptiness and sadness in their lives for more extended periods of time. Gorer feels that the loss of a child, especially an adolescent or young adult, causes a grief that never completely heals.

"During the days and weeks before death, when the dying person is in a conscious state, there are ways the people around him can help. Here are 10 commandments."

10 Commandments for Dealing with Death

Mary L. Meyer

Mary L. Meyer majored in journalism at the University of Minnesota and has taught high school.

Consider the following questions while reading:
1. **Does the author think terminally ill patients should be told that they are dying?**
2. **What "stages of death", that the dying experience, does the author describe?**
3. **What is the greatest fear many dying persons experience, in the opinion of the author?**
4. **Have you had an experience with a dying person that might suggest additional commandments?**

Victor Parsons, 41, construction worker, married for 20 years, father of two teen-age children, learned four years ago that he had an incurable disease.

Katherine Dodd, 28, college educated, bookkeeper for her husband's business, mother of an energetic three-year-old, has been hospitalized with an inoperable brain tumor.

Tom Rossoni, 17, high-school senior, honor student, letter-man in track, one of the most well-liked young men in his community, has suffered with an inherited Mediterranean blood disease all his life.

Different family backgrounds, different age groups and different daily activities, yet these people are likely to die slowly, probably after seemingly endless days in a hospital bed, from well-diagnosed life-draining diseases.

There are 300,000 new cases of terminal disease diagnosed each year in the United States. Although impending death is difficult for the dying person's family to adjust to, the awareness of death in the terminally-ill patient's life is the time when the need for his family is the greatest. During the days and weeks before death, when the dying person is in a conscious state, there are ways the people around him can help. Here are 10 commandments:

1. TELL THE PATIENT THAT HE IS DYING

Although families sometimes think it will be easier for the dying person if he is not told of his condition, the fact is that in many, if not most, cases, the terminally-ill patient knows he is going to die. He senses it in the way people act toward him —the increase in attention, or the tearful face of a relative, or the stumbling hesitancy of people who do not know what to say—all are clues to the sick person that he is going to die.

Regardless of the age of the dying person, he should know about his condition, because he will eventually discover the truth, anyway.

The parents of a 10-year-old boy who planned on not telling their son about his bone cancer were surprised one morning when he presented them with his written will, in which he expressed, among other things, the desire for his sister to have his tropical fish and his brother the baseball cards he valued so highly.

Even children over the age of six can comprehend the permanence and finality of death.

2. BE AWARE OF THE EMOTIONAL STAGES THE DYING PERSON EXPERIENCES

In her book, *On Death and Dying*, noted psychiatrist and author, Dr. Elisabeth Kubler-Ross, outlines five stages that the terminally-ill patient typically encounters. They are denial, anger, bargaining, depression and acceptance.

After denial and isolation, the dying person often becomes resentful. At this point, the patient might be angry at people, and at God, for his illness, and ask: "Why me? Why couldn't it have been somebody else who dies?"

On first learning of the seriousness of their malady, most patients deny the fact that their illness will result in death. The patient may believe there has been a mistake in diagnoses or a clerical error that means it will be somebody else who dies, not himself.

At the same time, the patient will try to isolate himself from his loved ones and hospital personnel who might remind him of his forthcoming death.

After denial and isolation, the dying person often becomes resentful. At this point, the patient might be angry at people, and at God, for his illness, and ask: "Why me? Why couldn't it have been somebody else who dies?"

This is a difficult stage for the family to deal with. The dying person often vents his frustrations in many ways. Take Victor Parsons, who, in the later stages of his terminal disease, became annoyed with the hospital staff because he was not allowed out of bed to go to the bathroom alone. When they did allow him to walk to the bathroom by himself, he was angry because he was not receiving enough personal attention from the nurses.

As the anger subsides, most patients have moments of bargaining. If being angry with God did not help, perhaps asking Him nicely for a longer life or days without pain will help. This bargaining often recurs at other stages in the person's illness. A woman with an advanced malignancy bargained to "live long enough to see her first grandchild," which she did. When she returned from the grandson's christening, she unconsciously tried to postpone her inevitable death by announcing that "there was another grandchild on the way."

As the disease progresses, treatments and hospitalization add up to financial worries and family problems that lead to a depression stage. If at all possible, the family should work together to alleviate some of these worries for the dying person. At this point, the depression also stems from the dying person's awareness that he is losing everyone and everything he loves. This is a time when the dying person is actually grieving his own death. Holding his hand, sitting quietly with him for a while or saying a prayer with him might be all he needs to see that you understand.

Toward the end, when the fear and anger have subsided, most dying patients reach a stage of acceptance. By this time, the patient may well be beyond talking about his death. But his family should still be at his side, even though the communication with him is now nonverbal.

Keep in mind that the terminally–ill patient might not enter these stages in this sequence, or that he might experience more than one stage simultaneously with another. The family should listen to the dying patient during these stages. If they can understand what he is going through, they can help him relieve the frustrations he feels.

3. DO NOT ISOLATE THE DYING PERSON

In numerous interviews, nearly every patient related that his greatest fear was not the dying itself, but dying alone. Yet, in hospitals and nursing homes, where 90 percent of deaths occur, dying patients are often placed in rooms at the end of the hall where they are farthest from the nurses' station.

One would think that doctors and nurses who come into contact with death every day would be well prepared to cope with dying patients, but studies in hospitals across the country find this is not so. Unfortunately, in American society, death has been a forbidden subject for so long that even medical personnel have unhealthy attitudes about it.

> *Non-verbal communication—a warm hand, a reassuring look in the eye, an encouraging smile—can relieve the dying person's loneliness.*

When asked why she tended to ignore the terminally-ill patients on her floor, one nurse replied: "I can't stand to talk about death, so I don't know what to say to them."

Often, especially when the person has reached the acceptance stage, he no longer wants to talk, but still needs to have frequent visits just to assure him of someone's presence, even if they do not converse verbally. Non-verbal communication—a warm hand, a reassuring look in the eye, an encouraging smile—can relieve the dying person's loneliness.

4. TALK ABOUT DYING WITH THE TERMINALLY-ILL PATIENT

Rare is the dying person who at some time does not want to discuss his illness. Most people, even children, want to learn about their sickness. They need to know what is happening within their bodies.

The strange hospital environment that the dying person is usually thrust into, with its unfamiliar faces, should not cut off communication. Allowing the dying person to grieve, to cry, to ventilate his emotions will not only make him feel more comfortable about his death but also make the adjustment less difficult for his family and the hospital personnel around him.

Talking about death is often difficult for the dying person, his family and hospital personnel at first, but, once the awkward beginnings are overcome, the experience of communicating can be gratifying to all involved. Reminiscing about the past might also afford an appreciation of the things the dying person still has to enjoy—at least in memory.

5. ENCOURAGE THE DYING PERSON TO TALK ABOUT HIS FEARS

When faced with death, a person develops anxieties that, if he were healthy, he would not even consider. These fears grow larger and larger in the patient's mind and are soon completely out of proportion.

For instance, a middle-aged woman was prolonging her own misery because she was unable to talk with anyone about her fear of lying underground in a cold, watery casket with worms eating her remains. After venting her fear to her son and discussing the problem, the son suggested entombment in a mausoleum as the solution to her fears of being underground. Shortly thereafter, the mother died, at peace with her fears.

Communication is the key to alleviating the problems of guilt, fear, anger, depression and loneliness that the dying person encounters.

6. TREAT THE DYING PERSON AS A PERSON

—not like a child or an invalid. The dying, as well as the healthy, need to be included in decisions. The entire family, children included, should be allowed to discuss the family's situation. Until death occurs, the terminally-ill person is part of his family and needs to feel that he still is.

In Tom Rossoni's case, his mother could not accept the fact that her son was dying. She felt guilty and blamed herself for his inherited blood disorder. She refused to discuss this with him. She waited on him constantly, disregarding any desires Tom had to adjust to the fact that he was dying. With the help of a hospital chaplain who helped her see that there was no way she could have prevented her son's illness, she was able to relieve herself of some of the guilt and to give her son the opportunity to mature. Only then did she accept the idea that she would lose him.

A good attitude or mental frame of mind can do more to prolong life than medicine can.

Include the dying person in decisions involving problems of family finances, discipline, career goals for the children and so on. This is important for the terminally-ill patient's mental well-being.

7. DO NOT BE AFRAID TO MAKE PLANS

If the dying person wants to talk about his will, funeral arrangements or what will happen to his family after his death, he certainly should have the opportunity to do so. To some people, this can mean the difference between an extended, agonizing death and a peaceful, contented death.

Husbands and wives should both know the status of their financial affairs, as well as the terms of any wills or trust funds they may have.

With the rising cost of funerals, funeral directors find that prearranged funerals are becoming increasingly popular. The family knows the approximate costs and type of funeral the dying person wants before the death occurs. Doing this sort of thing ahead of time takes a great deal of pressure off the family when their loved one actually dies.

Dying patients have a fear of leaving unfinished business. Take, for example, the case of a 60-year-old man who was afraid to die because his wife was a victim of Parkinson's disease and had no one else but him to take care of her. When the wife moved into a nursing home and her husband saw that she was in good hands, he was able to die peacefully.

Presumably, the family, particularly a wife or husband, is close enough to the dying person to ask outright: "Are you worried about what will happen to the rest of us after you're gone?" or "Do you want to make some funeral plans?" If they say "no," drop the subject with: "When you feel like talking about it, we will." This way the dying person knows he can reopen the discussion when he wants to.

8. DO THINGS NOW—
TOMORROW MAY BE TOO LATE

A dying person feels a sense of urgency. Each day counts, so he must finish things right away. It is not the big issues that matter so much to the dying person, but the little things. Katherine Dodd, when she learned of her serious illness and accepted it, immediately began writing letters for her daughter to read in the years after her death. She felt that was a way for her to "leave her daughter something to remember her by."

A dying patient frequently takes a stab at visible, earthly immortality by making items to give to friends and family or by writing letters to loved ones like Katherine Dodd did; in this way, the dying person shows that he wants to be remembered.

Do not take the attitude that the dying person is wasting his time or undertaking some project that is more than he can handle. Instead, encourage him. Give a helping hand if he asks for it. The time spent together may produce some pleasant memories for both people involved.

9. ENCOURAGE THE DYING PERSON TO MAINTAIN A FEELING OF HOPE

Even the most well-adjusted, realistic patient holds on to the possibility of discovering a last-minute cure for his illness. It may be a serious mistake to tell the dying person he has a certain number of months to live. Any doctor can tell of cases of patients who, from medical evidence, should have lived only two or three months but, instead, survived for a year or more.

A good attitude or mental frame of mind can do more to prolong life than medicine can.

10. LOOK TO THE DYING PERSON'S FAITH IN GOD FOR SOME ULTIMATE ORDER OF THINGS

Through the ordeal, both the dying person and his family can draw a great deal of strength from the Scriptures — or various inspirational literature and drama. Perhaps making his favorite music available to him and surprising him with an occasional gift of a new record, or keeping him supplied with his favorite kind of reading material will provide answers for the dying patient's troubled mind.

With the help of reassuring physicians and nurses who relay the feeling that everything possible is being done for him, a patient can rest easier.

If there is a clergyman acceptable to the patient, call on him to bring hope and meaning to the life of the patient.

The family that can make use of their resources to understand and accept the problem can also give the dying patient the outlook he needs to make his death peaceful...and dignified.

REACTING TO DEATH

Instructions

STEP 1

Each member of the class should try to remember the death of someone close — a relative, a friend or even a pet. Show how you reacted to this death by answering the following questions:

1. What feelings of grief did you experience?
2. How did you handle your grief?
3. How did other people help you overcome your grief?
4. Do you think that you will react the same way if someone else were to die soon? Why or why not?

STEP 2

Form into groups of four to six students. Compare your responses to the questions. Note the similarities and the differences in your answers.

STEP 3

Form new groups of four to six students. This time, be certain that each group has an equal number of male and female students. Compare your answers on the basis of sex. Do the responses of the young men differ from those of the young women? If there are differences between the two, what factors do you believe account for these differences?

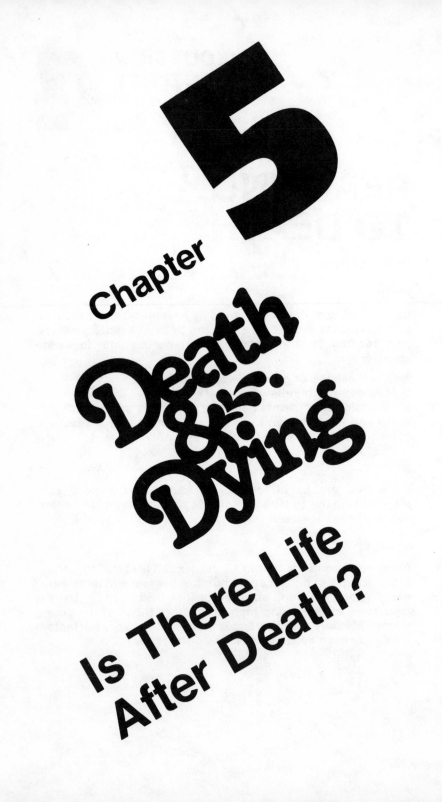

Chapter 5

Death & Dying

Is There Life After Death?

"I know for a fact there is life after death."

There is Life After Death

Elisabeth Kubler-Ross

In the publication of *On Death and Dying* in 1969, Dr. Elisabeth Kubler-Ross, the noted Swiss-born authority on the psychiatric aspects of terminal illness, spelled out five emotional stages dying patients experience—denial, anger, bargaining, depression, acceptance. She is founder/director of Shanti Nilaya, a healing center in Escondido, California.

Consider the following questions while reading:
1. **What evidence does the author present for the existence of life after death?**
2. **How does the author describe what life after death is like?**
3. **What is your opinion of the author's claim of life after death?**

"Life After Death? 'Yes Beyond a Shadow of Doubt', Says the Eminent Dr. Kubler-Ross". Reprinted with permission from November 24, 1975 issue *People Weekly*, © 1975 Time Inc. Text by Linda Witt.

When did you begin to think there is life after death?

I have always felt something significant happens a few moments after death. A minute or so after "clinical" death, most of my patients often got the most fantastically peaceful expressions, even those who had struggled terribly with death.

Any other indications?

I wondered, "To whom do people talk on their deathbeds?" My own father talked to his father who had been dead 30 years, and then turned back and spoke rationally to me. We label this "hallucination," as if once we superstitiously put a label on it, it is taken care of.

What would you describe as your first positive evidence?

About seven years ago, a patient who had been declared dead despite heroic last-minute resuscitation efforts spontaneously came alive three-and-a-half hours later. She shared with me how she felt: she had floated out of her physical body and watched herself being worked on. She described in minute detail the resuscitation team—who was there, who wanted to give up, who wanted to continue, who told a joke to relieve the tension. This gave me my first clue.

CASE HISTORY

One middle-aged man who had suffered a cardiac arrest related:

"I remember everything perfectly vividly. Suddenly I felt numb. As things began to fade, there was a sound I can't describe; it was like the beat of a snare drum, very rapid, a rushing sound, like a stream rushing through a gorge. After a second or two, I seemed to turn over and go up. It was dark — you could call it a hole or a tunnel — and there was this bright light. It got brighter and brighter. I seemed to go through *it.*

"All of a sudden I was...somewhere else. There was a gold light, everywhere. Beautiful. There was music. I seemed to be in a countryside with streams, grass, trees, mountains. The strangest thing was that there were people there. Not in any kind of form or body as we know it; they were just there."...

Raymond A. Moody, Jr., *Reflections on Life after Life.*

Have you found other similar cases?

Since then I have investigated similar cases from Australia to California, involving patients from age 2 to 96—I have 193 very clear-cut cases from all over the world, both religious and non-religious people. One had been "dead" 12½ hours. All experienced the same thing.

How did these people describe the experience of dying?

They virtually shed their physical bodies, as a butterfly comes out of a cocoon. They describe a feeling of peace, beautiful, indescribable peace, no pain, no anxiety. And they were perfect—completely whole. A young man whose leg was cut off in an automobile accident floated above the crash scene and observed the rescue effort, and recalls his leg being intact. They were so content that they resented, sometimes bitterly, the attempts to bring them back to life because they were coming back to a dreadful existence—cancerous bodies, amputated limbs. Not one of them was afraid to die again. The experience seems to be the same no matter what their cultural background.

You have mentioned that on his deathbed your father apparently spoke to his own dead father. Is there any pattern in the people dying patients seem to talk to?

Whomever you most loved in life who preceded you in death is there to help you make the transition, and you talk to them. It is a transition, as dramatic as cutting the umbilical cord. But the important thing is that you don't go through it alone. It is wonderful to be able to reassure parents of dying children: "Don't worry. There will be someone waiting to take care of your child."

If there is life after death, is there also heaven and hell?

After the transition, you achieve a higher understanding which includes a review of your own life. You see all the times you should have acted one way and acted another, all the times you regret. It is not God who has to convince you of your wrongs; it is you yourself, and it is hell.

Why and when did you decide to begin talking openly about life after death?

Initially I was afraid other scientists would say, "Oh, Ross has seen too many dying patients. She's slipped." But while I was answering questions after a speech last January, a woman whose small son had been declared dead and then revived, asked if there was something beyond death. I forgot the 1,000 others there and said, "I know for a fact there is life after death."...

AN ATHEIST'S FUNERAL

"All dressed up with no place to go."

Were you—and are you—religious?

I always joke that I am a wishy-washy Protestant, but I don't like such labels. Perhaps a better word is "spiritual," but it has nothing to do with life after death; it has to do with respect and appreciation for life. All the things people regard as tragedies—if you had multiple sclerosis or lost a best friend—these are gifts, virtual gifts, which help you understand the meaning of life. There are many kinds of loss besides death.

Has your conclusion that there is life after death changed you?

If I were to lose this house and everything in it, I virtually couldn't care less. Now, because of my work with dying patients, I know that to see a sunset or watch a pheasant family on the lawn are infinitely more important things. If you listen to dying patients say, "If only I had gotten to know my children. If only..." you begin to reflect on your own life.

How do you contemplate your own death?

I'm a fighter and basically a rebel. I don't know if I can die quietly and peacefully. I've learned, even though I can define five stages to death, that you can't write a cookbook, a recipe that will fit everyone. But if you know these things—that the stages of dying are not really about dying, but the way we learn to come to grips with the crisis of loss, any loss—you cannot possibly be afraid.

"If life after death could be empiri-cally verified 'beyond a shadow of a doubt,' then there would seem to be little need for faith. It would be the thanatologist rather than the believer who would inherit the kingdom of heaven."

A Christian Response to Kubler-Ross

Robert M. Herhold

Robert M. Herhold is pastor of Resurrection Lutheran Church in San Bruno, California.

Consider the following questions while reading:

1. What does the author mean when he says that Kubler–Ross substitutes reason for faith and believing with knowing?
2. Why does the theology of Kubler-Ross trouble the author?
3. The author claims that "life after death must be something other than more of the same". Do you agree?
4. What does he mean when he states that, for the Christian, the resurrection replaces immortality?

Robert M. Herhold, "Kubler-Ross and Life After Death". Copyright 1976 Christian Century Foundation. Reprinted by permission from the April 14, 1976 issue of *The Christian Century*.

ELISABETH KUBLER-ROSS, noted authority on death and dying, concluded a recent series of lectures before a group of clergymen at Pacific Grove, California, with these words: "I do not simply believe in life after death; I *know* that there is life after death." She expresses the same view in her book, *Questions and Answers on Death and Dying* (Macmillan, 1974): "Before I started working with dying patients, I did not believe in a life after death. I now believe in a life after death, beyond a shadow of a doubt" (p. 167).

In her lectures she told of accident victims whom doctors had pronounced dead, who then awoke and described the sensations they had experienced of being separate from, and floating blissfully above, their bodies. She also related an incident in which a young boy, though apparently dead, was revived by doctors. The boy, she said, told his mother: "I was dead and it was so beautiful I didn't want to come back. I was with Mary and Jesus. But Mary said, 'You have to go back, you have to save your mother.'"

GOD IS PROOF

In the last analysis, the chief proof of immortality is the character of God, and the belief that, however, we may conceive and define him, he is not so careless of human values as to create them only to destroy them just as they are beginning to understand and appreciate and achieve a little.

"The Everlasting Life" from *The Christian Century*, September 18, 1924.

Dr. Kubler-Ross indicated that these and other experiences with dying or "dead" patients have made her certain that there is a life after we die. Since her comments came at the conclusion of her sessions, no one questioned her at any length. Several pastors commented later on how reassuring her words were. At first I felt reassured too, but when I got home, my leg began to hurt where Dr. Kubler-Ross had pulled it. It was nice to hear that someone from another discipline had arrived, without benefit of clergy, at a belief in life after death. I was troubled, however, that Kubler-Ross had made not a statement of faith, but what she regarded as a statement of fact, "beyond a shadow of doubt."

FAITH NOT REASON

Kubler-Ross's certainty might be a welcome boost to the feeble faith of many Christians. But it does not seem to work that way for me. My leg is still sore. For me, her concept of immortality creates serious scientific, theological and biblical problems.

Life after death is, by definition, beyond the range of scientific research; it is in the realm of the extrasensory, not the sensory. If life after death could be empirically verified "beyond a shadow of a doubt," then there would seem to be little need for faith. It would be the thanatologist rather than the believer who would inherit the kingdom of heaven. Kubler-Ross would be the first to agree that faith is not a substitute for needed surgery or medication. Yet she appears to be substituting reason in an area where faith is needed.

The detached or objective researcher is essential to the scientific task. But who can remain detached or objective on the subject of death, particularly his or her own? The will to believe, or to make things believable, cannot escape even a mind of the stature of Kubler-Ross's. The trouble is that she confuses believing with knowing. I *believe* that Jesus Christ rose from the dead; I don't *know* that he did. If it were a matter of knowing, then research centers would be more appropriate than worship centers.

The "evidence" for life after death introduced by Kubler-Ross is scientifically unverifiable. Is a feeling of floating blissfully above one's body a statement of fact? If so, how do we go about verifying the experience? Anecdotal evidence is significant only to the person experiencing the event. It is evidence that cannot be proved to someone else as can the sum of two plus two.

THE THEOLOGY OF AFTERLIFE

Kubler-Ross's scientific methodology does not trouble me as much as her theology does. Nowhere do I get a hint that God may be what eternal life is all about. To be sure, many of us are more interested in having more time, or more creativity, or more of something else after death than we are in God. *But it is precisely the God question which concerned Jesus:* "And this is eternal life: for men to know you, the only true God, and to know Jesus Christ, whom you sent" (John

17:3, *Good News for Modern Man*). Life after death must be something other than more of the same, and that "other" is to know the love and wonder of God.

Even if Kubler-Ross convinces her audience that there is life after death, I wonder if they will really buy the idea. If our age is marked by meaninglessness and centerlessness, then the problem is only extended and enlarged by talking about more of the same. This is to cure boredom with the remedy of more time. On the other hand, if eternal life is life with God, then we are talking not simply in quantitative but in qualitative terms—not simply about more time but about a new relationship to all things. "Behold, I make all things new" (Rev. 21:15, RSV).

Cartoon reprinted from the *National Courier* Copyright 1977, Logos International Fellowship Inc., 201 Church Street, Plainfield, NJ and used by permission.

Many of us clergy are guilty of Kubler-Ross's error. *We try to relate people to life after death when we should be relating them to God.* It is the presence of God which gives eternal life its content. Paul does not celebrate our endless existence; rather he celebrates the fact that nothing can separate us from the love of God. Eternal life has meaning only to those who know something (the love of God) from which they do not want to be separated. Kubler-Ross and many of us are still hung up on immortality while Paul is talking about resurrection...

Kubler-Ross represents the view of many church people when she says: "I believe that our bodies die but the spirit or soul is immortal" (*Questions and Answers on Death and Dying,* p. 170). The problem is that immortality replaces the resurrection. One does not need Easter if the spirit or soul is immortal. But it is precisely because "when you're dead, you're dead" that the resurrection is such incredibly good news...

Kubler-Ross suggests a human-centered immortality fortified by stories of patients who have "died" and reported back. Other people like to think that God is a celestial Holiday Inn-keeper who has carefully filed their reservations. Another alternative is to believe that eternal life is to "know you, the only true God, and to know Jesus Christ, whom you sent."

DISTINGUISHING BETWEEN STATEMENTS THAT ARE PROVABLE AND THOSE THAT ARE NOT

From various sources of information we are constantly confronted with statements and generalizations about social and moral problems. In order to think clearly about these problems, it is useful if one can make a basic distinction between statements for which evidence can be found, and other statements which cannot be verified because evidence is not available, or the issue is so controversial that it cannot be definitely proved. Students should constantly be aware that social studies texts and other information often contain statements of a controversial nature. The following exercise is designed to allow you to experiment with statements that are provable and those that are not.

In each of the following statements indicate whether you believe it is provable (P), too controversial to be proved to everyone's satisfaction (C), or unprovable because of the lack of evidence (U). Compare and discuss your results with your classmates.

P = Provable
C = Too Controversial
U = Unprovable

_____ 1. We cannot rationally feel sorry for the departed person...because as dead, he is completely insensible to all such things as any piece of earth or non-living matter. He is just exactly as non-existent as he was before birth and conception.

_____ 2. Man is immortal. In _body_, through his children; in _thought_, through the survival of his memory; in _influence_, by virtue of the continuance of his personality as a force among those who come after him.

_____ 3. There is no total death. Only the body dies. The self or spirit, or whatever you may wish to label it, is eternal.

_____ 4. Everyone can tell when a person is definitely dead. But all the expertise in the world cannot tell when a person is still possibly alive.

_____ 5. The subjects of death and dying have largely been ignored as topics for open discussion.

_____ 6. We should not fear death, for then we cease to live life fully now.

_____ 7. Only the person who is incapable of loving another is entirely free of the possibility of grief.

_____ 8. A person who is dying _should_ be told that he/she is dying by a physician and/or by members of that person's family.

_____ 9. If life after death could be proved beyond a shadow of a doubt, then there would be little need for people to have faith.

_____ 10. A person never dies. His/her spirit goes through an endless cycle of rebirths.

"If we are to found our outlook of the world on what we discover in the scientific study of life, we are compelled to break with the notion that personality, individual identity, continues after death."

A Biological View of Life After Death

Herbert Spencer Jennings

Herbert Spencer Jennings (1868-1947) was a noted American scientist, educator and author. He taught zoology at Johns Hopkins University from 1906 to 1938. His numerous books include *Behavior of the Lower Organisms*, *The Biological Basis of Human Nature* and *The Universe and Life*.

Consider the following questions while reading:
1. **What does the evidence from biological science have to say about the existence of an afterlife?**
2. **Does the author see a conflict between religion and the scientific study of biology? Do you?**

Herbert Spencer Jennings, *The Universe and Life*. New Haven: Yale University Press, 1930. Reprinted with permission from the publisher.

In most forms of life, after a certain period of living, the existing individuals disappear; they die and are replaced by others.

This ceasing to live is an event that stands in sharp opposition to that striving for the promotion and fulness of his own life and that of his associates which is the mainspring of effort in each individual. Attempts have been made to convince the individuals that, in man at least, this change is only apparent; that, in fact, the same individuals continue to live after the event that we call death. Such a doctrine forms one of the main foundations of certain types of religion.

We are forced, I believe, to say that biological science finds no support for such a doctrine. Life does continue but in other individuals. It is toward fulness and adequacy and variety that life survives. But this is attained, perhaps quite as fully, or more fully, through the life of successive individuals as it would be through the continued life of the individual now in existence. Continued life of the present individuals would indeed avoid the process of aging and death, which casts a shadow on the life of those existing, and in so far works against the fulness and adequacy of life. But we are forced to take life as we find it, and what we find is that life consists not of indefinitely continuing individuals but of successive ones. No single individual of a later generation represents any single individual of a foregoing generation. For in the process of reproduction, the materials of life, the genes from many earlier generations, are thrown together, and from the mixture a new combination is extracted; so that each new individual represents or continues not one but many different individuals of foregoing generations. And no individual of a

---

A FOOLISH BELIEF

There is, perhaps, no more striking example of the credulity of man than the widespread belief in immortality. This idea includes not only the belief that death is not the end of what we call life, but that personal identity involving memory persists beyond the grave. So determined is the ordinary individual to hold fast to this belief that, as a rule, he refuses to read or think upon the subject lest it cast doubt upon his cherished dream.

Clarence Darrow, *Verdicts out of Court.*

---

later generation is found to continue the conscious personality of any individual of a previous generation, as the later hours of a single individual continue his earlier hours, through continuity or memory. 'Reproduction' is not reproduction alone, it is reproduction with a difference. The succeeding individuals are different combinations of materials, of genes, from any now existing. They have diverse characteristics, diverse characters, diverse personalities, from any that have before existed. And there is no evidence of the sort required for establishing the verifiable relations accepted in science that the individuals who have died still live as such in some other condition.

If then we are to found our outlook of the world on what we discover in the scientific study of life, we are compelled to break with the notion that personality, individual identity, continues after death. We are compelled to conclude that the individuals who have disappeared exist no more than they did before they began life, no more than they did before the species to which they belong had been produced in evolution. This I believe to be one of the fundamentals for a world outlook based on the study of biology.

"The mystery of the future is answered in the eternal of which we may speak in images taken from time...there is no time AFTER time, but there is eternity ABOVE time."

A Theological View of Life After Death

Paul Tillich

Paul Tillich was ordained in the Evangelical Lutheran Church in 1912. He taught philosophy and theology at several German universities until Nazism forced him to leave Germany in 1933. He taught at Union Theological Seminary, Harvard and the Divinity School of the University of Chicago. He died in 1965.

Consider the following questions while reading:
1. The author claims we are not completely within time. What does he mean?
2. Why does the author think that the common attitude about an endless future is an image of hell? Do you agree?
3. Do you agree with the author's claim that we should speak "about the eternal that is neither timelessness nor endless time" rather than life after death?

I am the Alpha and the Omega, the beginning and the end.
                                    REVELATION 21:6

It is our destiny and the destiny of everything in our world that we must come to an end. Every end that we experience in nature and mankind speaks to us with a loud voice: you also will come to an end! It may reveal itself in the farewell to a place where we have lived for a long time, the separation from the fellowship of intimate associates, the death of someone near to us. Or it may become apparent to us in the failure of a work that gave meaning to us, the end of a whole period of life, the approach of old age, or even in the melancholy side of nature visible in autumn. All this tells us: you will also come to an end.

WE BELONG TO ETERNITY

Whenever we are shaken by this voice reminding us of our end, we ask anxiously—what does it mean that we have a beginning and an end, that we come from the darkness of the "not yet" and rush ahead towards the darkness of the "no more"? When Augustine asked this question, he began his attempt to answer it with a prayer. And it is right to do so, because praying means elevating oneself to the eternal. In fact, there is no other way of judging time than to see it in the light of the eternal. In order to judge something, one must be partly within it, partly out of it. If we were totally within time, we would not be able to elevate ourselves in prayer, meditation and thought, to the eternal. We would be children of time like all other creatures and could not ask the question of the meaning of time. But as men we are aware of the eternal to which we belong and from which we are estranged by the bondage of time...

How do we react if we become aware of the inescapable end contained in our future? Are we able to bear it, to take its anxiety into a courage that faces ultimate darkness? Or are we thrown into utter hopelessness? Do we hope against hope, or do we repress our awareness of the end because we cannot stand it? Repressing the consciousness of our end expresses itself in several ways.

Many try to do so by putting the expectation of a long life between now and the end. For them it is decisive that the end be delayed. Even old people who are near the end do this, for they cannot endure the fact that the end will not be delayed much longer.

Many people realize this deception and hope for a continuation of this life after death. They expect an endless future in which they may achieve or possess what has been denied them in this life. This is a prevalent attitude about the future, and also a very simple one. It denies that there *is* an end. It refuses to accept that we are creatures, that we come from the eternal ground of time and return to the eternal ground of time and have received a limited span of time as *our* time. It replaces eternity by endless future.

Paul Tillich

ETERNITY ABOVE TIME

"The mystery of the future is answered in the eternal of which we may speak in images taken from time. But if we forget that the images are images, we fall into absurdities and self-deceptions. There is no time after time, but there is eternity above time."

But endless future is without a final aim; it repeats itself and could well be described as an image of hell. This is not the Christian way of dealing with the end. The Christian message says that the eternal stands above past and future. "I am the Alpha and the Omega, the beginning and the end."

THE ETERNAL NOW

The Christian message acknowledges that time runs towards an end, and that we move towards the end of that time which is our time. Many people—but not the Bible—speak loosely of the "hereafter" or of the "life after death." Even in our liturgies eternity is translated by "world without end." But the world, by its very nature, is that which comes to an end. If we want to speak in truth without foolish, wishful thinking, we should speak about the eternal that is neither timelessness nor endless time. The mystery of the future is answered in the eternal of which we may speak in images taken from time. But if we forget that the images are images, we fall into absurdities and self-deceptions. There is no time *after* time, but there is eternity *above* time...

It is hard for us to imagine our "being-no-more." It is equally difficult to imagine our "being-not-yet." But we usually don't care about our not yet being, about the indefinite time before our birth in which we were not. We think: *now* we are; this is *our* time — and we do not want to lose it. We are not concerned about what lies before our beginning. We ask about life after death, yet seldom do we ask about our being before birth. But is it possible to do one without the other? The fourth gospel does not think so. When it speaks of the eternity of the Christ, it does not only point to his return to eternity, but also to his coming *from* eternity. "Truly, truly, I say to you, before Abraham was, I *am*." He comes from another dimension than that in which the past lies. Those to whom he speaks misunderstand him because they think of the historical past. They believe that he makes himself hundreds of years old and they rightly take offense at this absurdity. Yet he does not say, "I *was*" before Abraham; but he says, "I *am*" before Abraham was. He speaks of his beginning out of eternity. And this is the beginning of everything that is — not the uncounted billions of years — but the eternal as the ultimate point in our past.

"Death is not final extinction for a Hindu, and has therefore no terrors for him...he knows that he does not live only once but goes through a cycle of births, deaths and rebirths till at last his individual soul merges into the universal soul."

AN EASTERN VIEW OF LIFE AFTER DEATH

Diwan Chand Sharma

Diwan Chand Sharma describes himself as a liberal and progressive Hindu and a member of a reformed sect of Hinduism. He is the author of *The Prophets of the East*.

Consider the following questions while reading:

1. What is the Hindu attitude toward death and reincarnation?
2. What is "Karma" and the Hindu doctrine of transmigration of the soul?

Diwan Chand Sharma, a personal letter to August Wagner. From August H. Wagner, *What Happens When You Die?* New York: Abelard-Schuman, 1968. Reprinted with permission from the author.

I was born in an orthodox Hindu family, and though I broke away early in life from some of the tenets of orthodoxy, to all intents and purposes I have remained a Hindu. At best I can describe myself a liberal and progressive Hindu, as one who is a member of a reformed sect of Hinduism. Though I have had very intimate relations with some members of the other faiths in India, I have not had any desire to change my faith. My attitude towards life as well as death is therefore coloured predominantly by what may be described as Hindu philosophy. When I say this I do not forget the fact that there are so many types and branches of Hindu philosophy.

In spite of so many diversities of outlook and speculation, I believe there is an underlying unity in Hinduism about the purpose of life and the meaning of death. I therefore write as an average Hindu, who is neither too sceptical nor too speculative, and who, without believing in any of the superstitions erroneously associated with Hinduism, still adheres to some of the grand and inspiring truths that Hindu religion in its purest form inculcates...

THE HINDU LIVES MORE THAN ONCE

Death is not final extinction for a Hindu, and has therefore no terrors for him. Life to him is the coming together of the body and the soul, and death to him is the dissolution of the body with the hope that his soul would migrate into another physical organism. He knows that he does not live only once but goes through a cycle of births, deaths and rebirths till at last his individual soul merges into the Universal Soul. This is the truth enunciated and affirmed in all the religious books of the Hindus, the Vedas, the Upanishads, the *Bhagavad Gita* and several others, and this is what is clearly imprinted on his mind. There are not perhaps many who attain to the final stage of salvation, but deep down on the mind of everyone is the truth of all this engraved...

TRANSMIGRATION OF THE SOUL

The average Hindu is a believer in the immortality of the soul. It may, however, be asked what happens to a man after death. To this question Yama gave a very conclusive answer to Nachiketas. He said that after death some beings are re-born as human beings, birds or animals, while others assume the forms of immovable objects such as trees. What kind of rebirth a person is going to have depends on his or her actions, or what is called 'Karma'. If a person's evil actions predominate over his good actions, he goes down in the scale of creation, but if there

128

is a balance of good actions in his favour, he rises in the scale of created things.

As it has been said by a recent historian of Indian philosophy, "Indian philosophers have from the very beginning discussed at great length the doctrines of the transmigration of the soul and the immortality of the soul, about which we find very little discussion in western systems of philosophy. The

EARTH A SCHOOLHOUSE

We may define reincarnation by saying that it is a plan whereby imperishable conscious beings are supplied with physical bodies appropriate to their stage of growth, and through which they can come in contact with the lessons of physical life.

From the standpoint of reincarnation the earth — and quite likely the whole universe — is a great school. It was brought into existence for educational purposes, and the whole plan of evolution is designed to give just the amount and kind of experience which is needed to stimulate the growth of an almost infinite series of living things, of which the known physical kingdoms form only a small part.

Just as a child goes to school day after day, learning lessons, gathering experience and passing from grade to grade, so do we in our greater soul-life come here to earth many times, learning lessons, gathering experience, and passing from one social grade to another.

Irving S. Cooper, *Reincarnation.*

doctrine of the transmigration of the soul is based on the theory of Karma or retribution, according to which rewards or punishments are given as fruits of the good or bad deeds done severally by man in their previous lives. Every man born here is sent by God to enjoy the fruits of his own deeds done in his past life, the doctrine of the transmigration of the soul has been part and parcel of most of the schools of Indian philosophy from the very earliest time. Their conception of *moksha* or final beatitude consists in freedom from the rounds of births and deaths and transmigration in this mortal world."

THE INEVITABILITY OF REBIRTH

Such is the Hindus' attitude toward death. He believes in the inevitability of death as he believes in the inevitability of rebirth. (For certain is death for the born, and certain is birth for the dead; therefore, over the inevitable thou shouldst not grieve — *The Bhagavad Gita*). He also knows that as a human being passes through childhood, adolescence and old age, in this body of his, similarly he migrates into another body after his death. Therefore, death to a Hindu is not like a "sleep that knows no waking". Nor is it annihilation. It does not also mean rotting in hell or enjoying oneself in heaven; for a Hindu the heaven or the hell is to be found in this world, where he reaps the fruit of his actions. Nor does a Hindu shut his eyes to this mystery. He does not believe like Confucius that since it is not possible to know all about life one should not probe into the mystery of death. He knows all about this mystery. He knows that he is like a tenant who after leaving one house goes straightaway to occupy another.

PETS AND PEOPLE

The pictures on this page and the next show tombstone inscriptions from two different cemeteries. One is a pet cemetery. The other is for people. Examine the inscriptions and then answer the questions on the following page.

QUESTIONS

1. What differences do you see in the inscriptions from the two cemeteries?

2. Why do you think that they are so different? Do you think that they are typical of these two kinds of cemeteries?

3. If a member of your family and your pet were to die, what tombstone inscriptions would you choose?

HELPFUL READINGS
MAGAZINE ARTICLES

Trevor Beeson — *Seeds of Resurrection: A Personal Reflection on Two Tragedies,* **Christian Century,** November 28, 1979, p. 1181.

Roy Branson — *Is Acceptance a Denial of Death? Another Look at Kubler-Ross,* **Christian Century,** May 7, 1975, p. 464.

Harry James Cargas — *Death Is Alone,* **Christian Century,** March 8, 1978, p. 230.

Catholic Bulletin — *No One Can Permit the Killing of an Innocent Human Being,* July 4, 1980, p. 10.

Ken Dychtwald — *Humanistic Gerontology,* **The Humanist,** July/August 1980, p. 26.

Leslie H. Farber — *O Death, Where Is Thy Sting-A-Ling?* **Commentary,** June 1977, p. 35.

John Garvey — *Death and Therapy,* **Commonweal,** July 22, 1977, p. 471.

Dennis J. Geaney — *Give in to Grief,* **U. S. Catholic,** February 1978, p. 11.

Daniel Goleman — *Back from the Brink,* **Psychology Today,** April 1977, p. 56.

We Are Breaking the Silence About Death, **Psychology Today,** September 1976, p. 44.

Carol K. Gross — *Death Is a Personal Matter,* **Newsweek,** January 12, 1976, p. 9.

Cornelia Holbert — *A Quiet Death with Dignity,* **America,** March 12, 1977, p. 214.

Human Behavior — *Dying Children: Candor about Certain Death,* March 1979, p. 49.

Walter Jeffko — *Redefining Death,* **Commonweal,** July 6, 1979, p. 394.

M. Kamien — *Death of a New Baby: The Grief No One Wants to Talk About,* **Glamour,** May 1979, p. 77.

Pattie Klein — *Madalyn Murray O'Hair: An Atheist Deals with Death,* **The American Atheist,** September 1978, p. 14.

Gerald Larue — *Death and the Humanist Counselor,* **The Humanist,** May/June 1980, p. 13.

P. MacDonald — *Death of a Parent: The Grief, the Guilt, the Anger... and the Growth,* **Glamour,** November 1979, p. 220.

Malachi B. Martin — *Life After Death,* **National Review,** March 17, 1978, p. 349.

Peter A. Metcalf	*Death Be Not Strange,* **Natural History,** June/July 1978, p. 6.
M. L. Meyer	*Dealing with Death,* **America,** August 27, 1977, p. 109.
Christopher F. Mooney	*Death and the Phenomenon of Life,* **America,** April 12, 1975, p. 276.
Ann Nietzke	*The Miracle of Kubler-Ross,* **Human Behavior,** September 1977, p. 18.
T. Organ	*Grief and the Art of Consolation,* **Christian Century,** April 1, 1979, p. 759.
James J. Preston	*Toward an Anthropology of Death,* **Intellect,** April 1977, p. 343.
R. Pucetti	*Experience of Dying,* **Humanist,** July 1979, p. 62.
Paul Ramsey	*The Indignity of "Death with Dignity",* **Hastings Center Studies,** May 1974, p. 56.
Parker Rossman	*Shadow Boxing with Death,* **The Christian Century,** April 23, 1980, p. 468.
Thomas Scheff	*Unresolved Grief,* **Center Magazine,** January/February 1980, p. 15.
R. Short	*Is Hell for Real?* **U. S. Catholic,** April 1980, p. 37.
Time	*Defining Death,* March 10, 1975, p. 76.
George F. Will	*A Good Death,* **Newsweek,** January 9, 1978, p. 72.
Kenneth L. Woodward	*Life After Death?* **Newsweek,** July 12, 1976, p. 41.
	Living with Dying, **Newsweek,** May 1, 1978, p. 52.

BOOKS

Tom L. Beauchamp and Seymour Perlin, eds.	**Ethical Issues in Death and Dying.** Englewood Cliffs, N.J.: Prentice-Hall, 1978.
Ernest Becker	**The Denial of Death.** New York: Free Press, 1973.
Nancy Doyle	**The Dying Person and the Family.** New York: Public Affairs Pamphlets, 1972.

Herman Feifel, ed.	**New Meanings of Death.** New York: McGraw-Hill, 1977.
Robert Fulton, et al	**Death and Dying: Challenge and Change.** Reading, Mass.: Addison-Wesley, 1979.
Earl Grollman, ed.	**Concerning Death: A Practical Guide for the Living.** Boston: Beacon Press, 1974.
	Talking About Death: A Dialogue Between Parent and Child. Boston: Beacon Press, 1978.
Paul E. Irion	**The Funeral: Vestige or Value?** Nashville: Abingdon Press, 1966.
Edgar N. Jackson	**When Someone Dies.** Philadelphia: Fortress Press, 1973.
Mark and Dan Jury	**Gramp.** New York: Grossman Publishers, 1976.
Stanley Keleman	**Living Your Dying.** New York: Random House, Berkeley: The Bookworks, 1974.
Elisabeth Kubler-Ross	**Death: The Final Stage of Growth.** Englewood Cliffs, N.J.: Prentice-Hall, 1975.
	On Death and Dying. New York: Macmillan, 1969.
	Questions and Answers on Death and Dying. New York: Collier Books, 1974.
Ignace Lepp	**Death and Its Mysteries.** New York: Macmillan, 1968.
Jessica Mitford	**The American Way of Death.** New York: Fawcett, 1963.
Raymond A. Moody	**Life After Life.** Harrisburg, Penn.: Stackpole Books, 1976.
Elizabeth Ogg	**A Death in the Family.** New York: Public Affairs Pamphlets, 1976.
Edwin S. Schneideman, ed.	**Death: Current Perspectives.** Palo Alto, Calif.: Mayfield Pub., 1976.
Michael A. Simpson	**The Facts of Death.** Englewood Cliffs, N. J.: Prentice-Hall, 1979.
Peter Steinfels and Robert M. Veatch	**Death Inside Out: The Hastings Center Report.** New York: Harper & Row, 1975.
Arnold Toynbee, et al	**Man's Concern with Death.** New York: McGraw-Hill, 1968.
Robert M. Veatch	**Death, Dying, and the Biological Revolution.** New Haven: Yale University Press, 1976.
Robert F. Weir, ed.	**Ethical Issues in Death and Dying.** New York: Columbia University Press, 1977.

JOURNALS

Death Education, Pedagogy, Counseling, Care. Hemisphere Publishing Corporation, 1025 Vermont Avenue N.W., Washington, DC 20005.

Essence, Issues in the Study of Aging, Dying, and Death. Atkinson College Press, 4700 Keele Street, Downsview, Ontario, Canada.

Journal of Thanatology. Alan R. Liss, Inc., 150 Fifth Avenue, New York, NY 10011.

Omega, The Journal of Death and Dying. Baywood Publishing Co., 43 Central Drive, Farmingdale, NY 11735.

Index

Jesus, 18-21, 23, 24, 66, 68, 81, 115-117
Jewish, 26-28
Johnston, Alva, 72

karma, 32, 127-129
Ketchel, Stanley, 72
Kubler-Ross, Elisabeth, 15, 62, 69, 73, 101, 114-117, viewpoints, 33-36, 109-113

livor mortis, 41

mechanical respirator, 41-44, 50, 61
medicolegal, 42
Mizner, Addison, 72
Mizner, Wilson, 72-73, 75-76
moksha, 129
mortality, 15, 24, 31, 60-65, 120-122
mourning, 86-89, 92-93, 96, 98

neocartex death, 44
nirvana, 32

Phillips, Wendell, 38
Plato, 78
pro-life movement, 46, 47

Raleigh, Sir Walter, 73, 75
reincarnation, 24, 30-32, 61, 127-130
resurrection, 19-21, 27, 61, 68-70, 117
resuscitation, 110
rigor mortis, 41

St. Augustine, 87, 124
senescence, 54
Shaw, George Bernard, 75
Sheol, 27
stream of consciousness, 31-32

terminally-ill, 100-106
thanatologist, 114, 116
Thomistic philosophy, 47
Thoreau, Henry David, 74
Tibetan Book of the Dead, 30
transcendentalist, 74
transmigration, 32, 127-129
transplantation, 41-44, 51
Truman, Harry S., 38

Yama, 32, 128

ACKNOWLEDGMENTS

Illustrations and Picture Credits

Page

14   David L. Bender

35   Courtesy of Shanti Nilaya

64   Courtesy of Mell Lazarus and Field Newspaper Syndicate

74   © G. B. Trudeau

82   David L. Bender

90   Courtesy of Grief Center, Burnsville, Minnesota

112   John Cade

117   © Logos International Fellowship, Inc.

125   Courtesy of University of Chicago

131,
132   David L. Bender

MEET THE EDITORS

David L. Bender is a history graduate from the University of Minnesota. He also has a M.A. in government from St. Mary's University in San Antonio, Texas. He has taught social problems at the high school level for several years. He is the general editor of the Opposing Viewpoints Series and has authored most of the titles in the series.

Richard Hagen received his B.A. in history and political science from St. Olaf College and a B.S. degree in social studies education from the University of Minnesota. He has taught high school social studies and also has experience in journalism and advertising. He has developed a number of materials for Greenhaven Press.

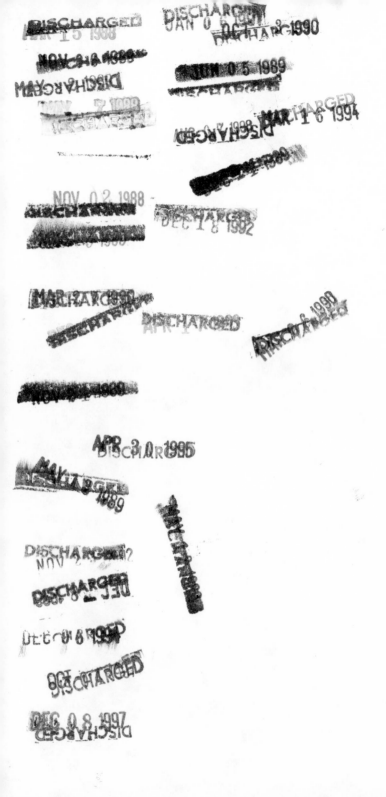